YVETTE VAN BOVEN

HOME MADE
IN THE OVEN

TRULY EASY, COMFORTING RECIPES
FOR BAKING, BROILING, AND ROASTING

ABRAMS, NEW YORK

Editor: Sarah Massey
Production Manager: Denise LaCongo

Library of Congress Control Number: 2019930873

ISBN: 978-1-4197-4044-2
eISBN: 978-1-68335-754-4

ABRAMS The Art of Books
195 Broadway, New York, NY 10007
abramsbooks.com

PLUM VLAAI, PAGE 141

CONTENTS

INTRODUCTION

VEGETABLES

FISH & MEAT

BAKING

INDEX

RECIPES BY MONTH

APPLE TARTLETS, PAGE 181

A COUPLE OF THINGS

ABOUT THE OVEN

These days I cook in a gas oven, after having used a convection one for years. By now I have built up a lot of experience with my gas oven and I know exactly how much hotter I need to stoke it in order to achieve the same result as in an electric oven.

I have a good-quality oven thermometer. It's clamped onto the rack inside the oven, and it's there that I determine my oven temperature rather than by the temperature on the oven itself. The temperature you set your oven to—visible on the dial or a digital display—doesn't necessarily correspond to the inside actual temperature. To accurately gauge this temperature you need an oven thermometer. For just a few bucks, you can buy one at any cooking or home goods store.

Each oven bakes differently. Some run hotter, other ones are slower. Even between ovens from the same brand there can be significant differences. This means your oven can take shorter or longer than the cooking times I suggest in the recipes. For this reason, I mention an *average oven temperature* in my recipes. Hence the cooking times in this book should be used as *suggestions*.

It's best to rely on your own experience with your own oven. Always check your dish, preferably slightly before the suggested cooking time, to see how it's coming along and then decide for yourself whether to take it out or to bake it a little longer.

Once you have really gotten the hang of your oven, you will start using it more often. I cook at least half of my dishes in mine. Often more than one at a time. This way I keep my hands free to do other stuff in the meantime.

ABOUT MEASUREMENTS

1 tablespoon = 15 ml
1 coffee spoon = 7 ml
1 teaspoon = 5 ml

Preferably use measuring spoons (those sets found in cookware stores) and common sense. Also, do taste as well; you will be the one who has to eat it later, so if you prefer something a little sweeter, saltier, zestier, or spicier than my recipe calls for, simply adjust the seasoning accordingly.

ABOUT INGREDIENTS

Your choice of good-quality ingredients can make or break the magnificent taste of your recipes. For instance, buy the tastiest olive oil or butter (no margarine—yuck!) you can afford. You will really taste the difference. For the same reason, use home-made rather than store-bought stock. Make it by steeping vegetable trimmings or bones and carcasses, leftover after a meal. Keep them in a bag in the fridge and make a broth once every couple of days while you're cooking, as you are busy in the kitchen anyway. It's hardly any work and you'll be throwing away less food too. Broths can always be stored in the freezer for later use.

Everyone should decide for him- or herself which meat to buy. I used to be more prescriptive and always include the word "organic" in my ingredients lists. But not everyone has the same ideals I do, and I know that organic meat from a reliable source is a lot more expensive. Therefore, my motto is: Eat meat less often, and when you do eat it, buy organic meat from animals that had been raised sustainably. That's how I do it: better for both animals and the planet.

One last thing: I use organic eggs size M (for "medium"), the standard size found in the supermarket.

ZUCCHINI FRITTATA WITH 'NDUJA, PAGE 119

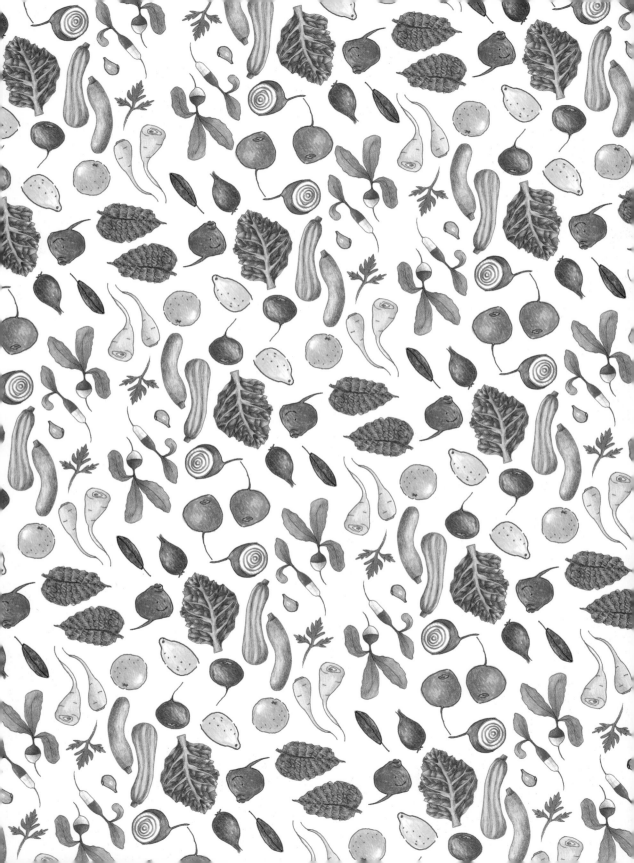

VEGETABLES

EAT MORE VEGETABLES

WITH CREAM...

AND CHEESE,

AND RICOTTA TOO,

IT SHOULD BE DOABLE

This dish pairs nicely with the meatballs from page 91, but it works just as well as a stand-alone dish, served with a good salad. Serve in soup bowls as single portions and it will immediately look like a serious dinner. As if you really made an effort. Since most of us are eating a little less meat these days, I will give you even more inspiration for vegetable dishes in this book. So off we go, and remember: Anything made in the oven with cream and cheese will be a surefire hit with almost everyone. Even my hubby, Oof, normally not a fan of sweet potatoes, gobbled up two portions. Who's next?

SWEET POTATO & SPINACH GRATIN

serves 4

- 1 cup plus 1 tablespoon (250 ml) heavy cream
- 1 clove garlic, peeled and crushed
- 2 sprigs fresh thyme
- 2 tablespoons olive oil
- 14 ounces (400 g) spinach
- Sea salt and freshly ground black pepper
- Freshly grated nutmeg
- 1 pound 14 ounces (850 g) sweet potatoes, peeled
- Butter for the baking dish
- Generous 1 cup (250 g) ricotta
- Scant ⅔ cup (60 g) grated aged cheese, such as Parmesan

Preheat the oven to 400°F (200°C).

In a saucepan, bring the cream, garlic, and thyme sprigs to just under a boil and let steep at that temperature for 10 minutes. Remove and discard the garlic and thyme.

In a wok, heat the oil and briefly stir-fry the spinach. Season with salt, pepper, and nutmeg. Press the spinach in a strainer to remove excess liquid.

Very thinly slice the sweet potatoes with a mandolin or a food processor.

Butter a baking dish and spread one-quarter of the potato slices in the bottom. Spread some of the ricotta on top and season with salt and pepper. Place a second layer of potatoes on top, then ricotta, pepper, salt, and spinach, and continue layering until everything has been used. Douse with the cream. Sprinkle with the grated cheese and bake for 45 minutes, or until everything is nicely done.

CUBE A GENEROUS
AMOUNT OF BUTTERNUT
SQUASH & RUTABAGA
AND ROAST THEM

SAUTÉ
SHALLOT, • RICE ← GARLIC
+
SAGE
IN BUTTER

DOUSE
WITH
WINE

AND
VEGE-
TABLE
BROTH

MIX IN SOME
CHEESE

→→→ COOK IN THE OVEN FOR A WHILE ←←←

Perhaps you're like me and you have had it with the culinary
fuss. This is simple food that can be eaten with just a spoon
and in which you can use those vegetables from the produce
drawer of your fridge as well as those holiday cheese leftovers.
There is no dish more comforting than a bowl of risotto. And
because this one comes out of the oven, it requires only a
little work. After just 10 minutes of tinkering in the kitchen
you can go straight back to the couch you came from. If only
every day could be this cozy.

BUTTERNUT SQUASH RISOTTO WITH SAGE

Preheat the oven to 400°F (200°C).

Spread the vegetable cubes out on a baking sheet and sprinkle
with a splash of oil and some salt and black pepper. Roast for
30 minutes, until they start to brown. For the last 10 minutes,
place a baking dish in the oven as well so it can preheat.

Meanwhile, melt the butter in a nonstick skillet. Add the
shallots and stir-fry for 6 minutes, until soft. Stir in the rice,
sage, and garlic, stirring every other minute or so.

Spoon in the roasted vegetables and three-quarters of the
cheese and douse with the wine. Stir everything loose until
it's thoroughly mixed.

Reduce the oven temperature to 350°F (180°C) and spoon
the vegetable mixture into the warm baking dish. Pour in
the hot broth and stir well once more. Bake uncovered for
40 minutes.

Serve right away with the rest of the cheese sprinkled on top.

serves 4

½ butternut squash, peeled
and cut into ⅜-inch (1 cm)
cubes

½ rutabaga or another root
vegetable, peeled and cut
into ⅜-inch (1 cm) cubes

Splash of olive oil

Sea salt and freshly ground
black pepper

Knob of butter
(about 1 tablespoon)

2 shallots, minced

1½ cups (300 g) arborio rice

1 small bunch fresh sage, cut
into slivers

2 cloves garlic, pressed

¾ cup (75 g) grated Parmesan
or another cheese (for on
top)

¾ cup plus 1 tablespoon
(200 ml) dry white wine

4½ cups (1 L) hot vegetable
broth

COMBINE IN A PITCHER:

TWO CANS OF DICED TOMATOES, & SPICES SUCH AS CUMIN, CINNAMON, SMOKED PAPRIKA POWDER, CAYENNE & OREGANO

IN A PAN: SAUTÉ

ONION, GARLIC, JALAPEÑO

SWEET POTATO

SPINACH & BLACK BEANS

TWIST OF LEMON

+ HALF OF THE SAUCE IN THE PITCHER

SPOON THE SAUCE ONTO SMALL TORTILLAS. ROLL UP AND INTO A DISH THEY GO. SAUCE & CHEESE ON TOP & **BAKE**

Let's make a fresh and clean start in January. I was thinking: vegetarian and comforting. When it comes to flavor, corn tortillas are my wholehearted preference over flour. When I discovered that my neighborhood supermarket sold them in their gluten-free section, I immediately stocked up on them. Not only do they taste better than flour tortillas, but they're also a bit lighter, just as sweet potatoes are somewhat lighter than regular potatoes. Starting the year off nice and light, using only vegetables: it just feels like a good idea to use tortillas made from vegetables too.

VEGETARIAN ENCHILADAS

Preheat the oven to 400°F (200°C).

Make the sauce: Combine all the ingredients in a pitcher.

In a large saucepan, sauté the onion in the oil until tender, add the garlic, and cook for another minute.

Stir in the jalapeños and sweet potatoes and cook, covered, for 12 to 15 minutes, until done, stirring occasionally. Spoon in half of the sauce, the spinach, and the beans. Let simmer and reduce to a "non-wet" filling. Season with lime juice.

Fill each tortilla with a scoop of filling and roll up. Pack the rolls side by side in a greased baking dish.

Pour the remaining sauce on top and sprinkle with the cheese. Bake for about 20 minutes, until the cheese is golden brown and the sauce bubbling.

Garnish with cilantro and avocado chunks. Serve with some sour cream.

TO GARNISH

Fresh cilantro, finely chopped

Avocado chunks

Sour cream

serves 4

FOR THE SAUCE

2 (14.5-ounce/411 g) cans diced tomatoes

1 tablespoon ground cumin

2 teaspoons dried oregano

1 teaspoon ground cinnamon

1 teaspoon smoked paprika

¼ teaspoon cayenne pepper

Sea salt and freshly ground black pepper to taste

AND ALSO

1 onion, finely chopped

1 tablespoon olive oil

4 cloves garlic, finely chopped

1 to 2 tablespoons finely chopped jalapeños

2 sweet potatoes, peeled and finely diced

7 ounces (200 g) spinach

1 (15.5-ounce/439 g) can black beans, rinsed and drained

Squeeze of lemon juice

12 small (or 6 large) corn tortillas, briefly heated

1 cup (100 g) shredded cheese

PEEL
ROOT VEGETABLES

GRATE WITH THE
COARSE GRATER PLATE
IN THE FOOD PROCESSOR

COMBINE WITH
EGG, CHEESE
& HERBS

PRESS MIXTURE INTO
THE GREASED CUPS
OF A MUFFIN PAN

... ——➤ and bake! ◀—— ...

Recently I was looking for a side dish to substitute for potatoes because I had run out of those. What I did find in my produce drawer were half a celeriac and a lonely sweet potato. I didn't expect to actually feed six people with this meager amount, but in fact it was easy. And what's more, I thought my root concoction looked pretty restaurant-ish.

This is a recipe to keep handy, pinned to your fridge, because you could make this using any root vegetable and cheese you have lying around. You'll always have a nice side dish on hand. Serve these tartlets with a large bowl of salad and a roasted chicken or fish and you'll be sitting down to a fantastic dinner just like that.

ROOT VEGETABLE TARTLETS

Preheat the oven to 400°F (200°C).

Grate the celeriac and sweet potato on the coarse holes of a box grater or in a food processor with the coarse grater plate. Mix with the lemon juice right away to prevent discoloration.

Using clean hands, mix in the sage, eggs, and cheese until evenly combined. Season with a pinch of salt and a generous amount of pepper.

Thoroughly grease a muffin pan with twelve cups and divide the vegetable mixture among the cups. Press carefully until the surface is nicely even. Bake the tartlets for 35 to 40 minutes, until nicely golden brown and done.

Still in doubt about the doneness? You should be able to pierce them with a sharp knife. If you feel any resistance that means they need to stay in the oven for a little longer. Done baking? Turn them out of the muffin pan and serve as a side dish right away.

serves 6 as a side dish

½ celeriac, cleaned (about 12 ounces/350 g)

1 sweet potato (8¾ ounces/ 250 g), also cleaned

Juice of ½ lemon

Handful of sage leaves, chopped (or oregano or rosemary)

4 eggs

½ cup (50 g) grated Parmesan cheese

Sea salt and freshly ground black pepper

Splash of olive oil for the pan

AU!

CUT OFF THE
PUMPKIN'S CAP
& HOLLOW OUT.

FRY SPINACH
& AN ONION

IN A WIDE BOWL,
LET COOL BRIEFLY.

ADD
MASCARPONE,

SOME
GOAT CHEESE

HANDFULL
OF BREADCRUMBS.

FILL THE PUMPKIN
WITH THE STUFFING.
BRUSH WITH SOME
OLIVE OIL.
COOK FOR 1 HOUR.
SERVE WITH
THE CAP ON TOP,
OF COURSE

In December I was doing book signings in bookstores throughout the Netherlands. It was close to Christmas and people were lining up in remarkably long lines in order to personalize their cookbook gifts with my signature. I'm not telling you this to brag about myself, but rather about Ceder, a boy who was standing in line with his mother and his big brother. He had already sent me a postcard once and now he had traveled for an hour and stood in line for another hour just to shake my hand. Once it was his turn, he handed me a beautiful baby pumpkin. He was nervous, so he didn't say much, but such a cheerful, round pumpkin says more than a thousand words. I promised him that I'd use it to cook something delicious and animal-free, because he doesn't eat animals. Voilà, Ceder, see you soon.

FiLLED BABY PUMPKiN

Preheat the oven to 400°F (200°C).

Cut off the pumpkin's cap. Remove the seeds and pulp using a knife and a tablespoon. Sprinkle with salt and pepper.

Slightly sauté the onion in the oil until tender, then add the spinach as well. Let cool in a bowl. Now add the rest of the ingredients and stir until the filling is evenly combined. Use it to stuff the pumpkin.

Oil the outside of the pumpkin, as well as a baking dish. Place the pumpkin and its cap side by side in the dish, cover with aluminum foil, and bake for 45 minutes. Remove the foil and bake for 15 minutes more. You can eat it whole.

for 1 boy

1 small organic pumpkin (about 1 pound 9 ounces/700 g)

Sea salt and freshly ground black pepper

1 onion, finely chopped

2 tablespoons olive oil, plus extra

10½ ounces (300 g) spinach

⅓ cup (75 ml) mascarpone cheese

½ cup (50 g) crumbled goat (or other) cheese

Generous ⅓ cup (30 g) panko or regular breadcrumbs

Pinch of red pepper flakes

HEAT MILK, BUTTER & SALT.

ADD SE-MO-LINA: STIR!

ADD PARMESAN AND EGG YOLKS

AND THEN...

POUR ONTO A BAKING SHEET, LET COOL UNTIL FIRM

OR ROLL UP. THE MIXTURE IN BETWEEN PARCHMENT PAPER, LET FIRM UP & CUT SLICES USING A WET KNIFE.

CUT OUT ROUNDS.

SHINGLE THEM IN AN OVEN DISH ♥ SPRINKLE WITH CHEESE

AND BAKE

Semolina can be used for more than making traditional Dutch *griesmeel* pudding. In Rome they also know their way with it. The Romans use it for a savory dish that I would love to share with you here. The texture of *gnocchi alla romana* is very similar to that of polenta. But since we are using semolina, made from durum (a hard wheat variety), instead of cornmeal, it's a bit different—lighter. We ate this dish with a thick, spicy tomato sauce and a bowl of salad. Delicious comfort food for a cold day. And afterward you can eat one of those little puddings for dessert, you know, with some cranberry sauce poured on top.

serves 6 as a side dish

4½ cups (1 L) whole milk

5 tablespoons plus 1 teaspoon (75 g) butter

Sea salt

1⅓ cups (250 g) semolina

1 cup (100 g) finely grated Parmesan cheese, plus extra

2 egg yolks

Freshly ground black pepper

Splash of olive oil

GNOCCHI ALLA ROMANA

In a large saucepan, bring the milk, butter, and a pinch of salt to a boil and turn the heat to medium-high. Whisk in the semolina and cook for 1 to 2 minutes, until it has thickened and is fiercely bubbling. Remove from the heat and stir in the cheese and egg yolks. Season with salt and pepper.

Pour the thick batter in two portions onto two large sheets of parchment paper and use these papers to swiftly shape it into two thick rolls. (Or pour onto a parchment paper–lined baking sheet and smooth the surface using the back of a wet spoon.)

Let cool completely. Once it has reached room temperature, put in the refrigerator. Let firm up for at least 2 hours; you could do this a day in advance.

Preheat the oven to 400°F (200°C).

Using a wet knife, cut the roll into ½-inch (12 mm) slices, or use a round cutter to cut discs from the dough sheet. Oil a baking dish and shingle the slices in the dish. Sprinkle with extra cheese and some oil. Bake for 25 to 30 minutes, until golden brown and piping hot.

 (VEGETABLE) MASH LEFTOVERS? NO PROBLEM!

 USE IT TO BAKE BREAD.

 SOAK YEAST IN LUKE-WARM MILK

ADD

 COMBINE MASH, EGG, SOFT BUTTER & SALT

 ADD FLOUR & AS MUCH MILK AS NECESSARY

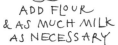 LET RISE

 PRESS THE DOUGH INTO A GREASED BAKING SHEET. SPRINKLE WITH SALT & DECORATE WITH CABBAGE LEAVES FOR IN-STANCE (OR NOT!) LET RISE BRIEFLY AND BAKE!

We recently ate Dutch potato-vegetable mash on a day when the weather was gloomy—I was actually looking for an excuse to eat smoked sausage, so I chose a dish to go with it. We had just a bit left; not quite enough for the day after, and it would be a shame to simply throw it out. Suddenly I remembered my own old recipe for potato focaccia made with mashed potatoes; potatoes are the bomb when used in bread. They make it soft and spongy, and it becomes a comforting kind of bread that you'd want to eat every day. I hoped it would pair well with the mash. The result was surprisingly good. Hurray, we repurposed another leftover dish and we ate a delicious bread that night. A perfect solution.

serves 4

- 2¼ teaspoons (one 7 g envelope) instant yeast
- 1 cup plus 1 tablespoon (250 ml) lukewarm milk
- 8¾ ounces (250 g) potato-vegetable mash, or mashed potatoes, at room temperature
- ⅔ cup (1 stick plus 3 tablespoons/150 g) butter, at room temperature
- 2 eggs
- 1 teaspoon salt
- 4¾ cups plus 2 tablespoons (625 g) all-purpose flour, plus extra
- 2 to 3 tablespoons olive oil
- Sea salt flakes

LEFTOVER FOCACCIA

Dissolve the yeast in 3 tablespoons of the milk.

Combine the mash, butter, eggs, and salt until smooth. Add the yeast mixture and the rest of the milk. Mix well. Stir in the flour. Knead for at least another 5 minutes with flour-dusted hands. Shape into a nice supple ball and set the dough in a warm spot for at least 1 hour to rise.

Knead the dough for another 3 minutes on a flour-dusted countertop, and press the dough into a large, oval, flat loaf of about 8 by 12 inches (20 by 30 cm).

Line a baking sheet with parchment paper and dust with flour. Set the dough on the parchment. Brush lightly with oil and sprinkle with some salt flakes. Cover with a clean dish towel.

Preheat the oven to 400°F (200°C).

Let the bread rise for another 30 minutes, then bake for 25 to 30 minutes, until golden brown.

COOK QUINOA
(PRONOUNCED
"KEEN-WAH")

ROAST
BROCCOLI

TOAST
WALNUTS

THOROUGHLY
COMBINE EVERYTHING
WITH CHEESE, CHILE
FLAKES, GARLIC,
SALT & MILK OR BROTH.

SPOON INTO OVEN DISH,
SPRINKLE WITH MORE
CHEESE & NUTS
AND BAKE IT!

I recently read in the Dutch newspaper *De Volkskrant* that the consumption of quinoa in the Netherlands is on the rise. This surprised me, really. I thought the hype was long over. I like quinoa very much; it's a bit nutty, and crispy in a salad or as a side dish. However, I actually had stopped buying it after I heard stories about the Peruvian people (the plant is native to the Andes mountains) who are no longer able to afford it due to our huge consumption. But from that Dutch article I learned that quinoa is now being grown by Dutch farmers (organically) and that the price for the Peruvians has leveled— a relief. That evening I immediately made a dish with Dutch quinoa. It's nutritious, rich in fibers, minerals, and proteins, and gluten free, in case that's important to you. It's an ideal substitute for potatoes or rice, only much lighter.

serves 4

¾ cup plus 2 tablespoons (150 g) quinoa (any color)

Scant 2 cups (450 ml) vegetable stock or water

1 pound 7 ounces (650 g) broccoli florets (2 heads)

4 tablespoons (60 ml) olive oil, plus extra for greasing the baking dish

Sea salt and freshly ground black pepper

Pinch of red pepper flakes

1 clove garlic, pressed

1½ cups (150 g) shredded cheese, such as Cheddar or Gouda

About 1 cup plus 1 tablespoon (250 ml) vegetable stock or milk

Handful of shelled walnuts

QUINOA & BROCCOLI FROM THE OVEN

Preheat the oven to 400°F (200°C).

Cook the quinoa for 20 minutes in the scant 2 cups (450 ml) stock or water until all the liquid has been absorbed. Remove from heat and let evaporate for 10 minutes.

Combine the broccoli with 2 tablespoons of the oil, and salt and pepper to taste, and arrange on a baking sheet lined with parchment paper. Roast for 20 minutes.

Toast the walnuts in a dry skillet until crunchy. Break them into pieces.

Lower the oven temperature to 350°F (180°C). Mix the cooked quinoa with salt, pepper, red pepper flakes, garlic, two-thirds of the cheese, and the 1 cup plus 1 tablespoon (250 ml) stock or milk until thoroughly combined.

Fold in the broccoli florets until they're entirely coated. Scoop this into a greased baking dish and sprinkle with the remaining cheese and the walnuts. Bake the dish for 25 minutes.

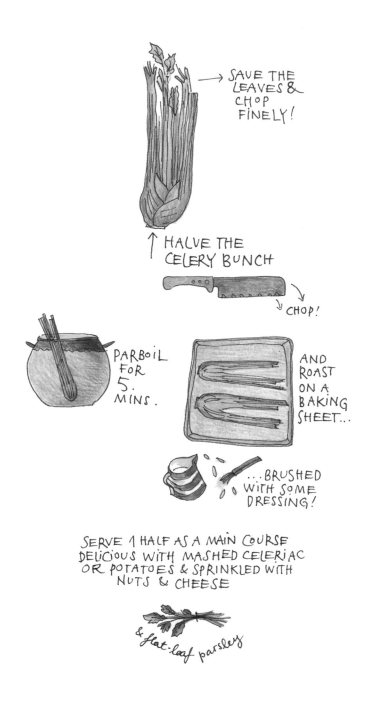

SAVE THE LEAVES & CHOP FINELY!

↑ HALVE THE CELERY BUNCH

↳ CHOP!

PARBOIL FOR 5. MINS.

AND ROAST ON A BAKING SHEET...

...BRUSHED WITH SOME DRESSING!

SERVE 1 HALF AS A MAIN COURSE DELICIOUS WITH MASHED CELERIAC OR POTATOES & SPRINKLED WITH NUTS & CHEESE

& flat-leaf parsley

After a couple of extravagant days in Paris and Antwerp, it was really time for reflection in Van Boven's kitchen. All this feasting really needed to be over. From now on, simplicity is the mantra. Well that's easier said than done; I have to constantly test recipes and then, what to do with all that food? Best to eat it, but doing that you turn fat. Sharing is the solution. Bringing people together for a simple dinner—that's fun.

Slow-roasted celery is such a simple thing, so bare-bones but at the same time such an amazing dish. It's exciting and full of flavors that compete for attention. It's as if you're eating three courses at the same time, but in one simple dish. Oh, simplicity is such fun.

serves 4

Sea salt

2 bunches celery, halved lengthwise, leaves coarsely chopped

3 to 4 cloves garlic, pressed

3 tablespoons apple cider

6 tablespoons (90 ml) hazelnut oil or good olive oil

Freshly ground black pepper

1 bunch fresh parsley, coarsely chopped

¾ cup plus 1 tablespoon (200 ml) vegetable stock, acidified with 2 to 3 tablespoons apple cider

Heaping 1 cup (150 g) crumbled blue (Stilton) cheese

⅔ cup (70 g) coarsely chopped hazelnuts

ROASTED CELERY

Preheat the oven to 400°F (200°C).

Bring a large pot of salted water to a boil. Blanch the celery for 3 minutes, scoop them out with a slotted spoon, and let drain. Place the celery on a baking sheet, cut sides down.

Whisk the garlic with the cider and oil and season with salt and pepper.

Sprinkle the celery with half of the dressing and half of the parsley and slide the baking sheet into the oven. Pour the stock over them and cook for 45 to 60 minutes (depending on the thickness of the celery), until it's al dente and the tips are coloring.

Transfer to a serving platter if desired. Drizzle with the rest of the dressing; sprinkle with the rest of the parsley, the celery leaves, cheese, and hazelnuts; and serve.

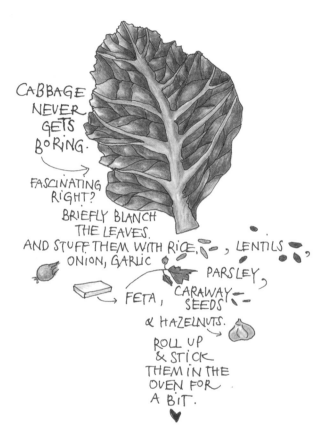

CABBAGE
NEVER
GETS
BORING.

FASCINATING
RIGHT?

BRIEFLY BLANCH
THE LEAVES.
AND STUFF THEM WITH RICE, , LENTILS ,
ONION, GARLIC
PARSLEY,
FETA, CARAWAY
SEEDS
& HAZELNUTS.

ROLL UP
& STICK
THEM IN THE
OVEN FOR
A BIT.

Well, I've ordered seeds and my new vegetable garden is almost finished. It was quite a bit of work, because we built raised beds from scratch. Soon I'll be growing the most diverse vegetables, ones that I never see at the farmers' market in the Netherlands (otherwise I'd buy them). There will be red broad beans, long white string beans, and black radishes in my vegetable beds.

But first we'll finish enjoying the last of the winter vegetables. You may be quite done with cabbage, but prepared this way, it becomes tempting again.

CABBAGE ROLLS WITH CARAWAY & HAZELNUT

Heat a splash of oil in a pan with a lid. Sauté the onion with the garlic until tender. Add the rice and lentils. Douse with 1⅔ cups (400 ml) of the stock and bring to a boil. Lower the heat, place the lid on the pan, and let simmer gently for 25 minutes, or until the lentils are al dente. Let everything cool off for a bit.

Blanch the cabbage leaves in salted water, rinse well, and remove the tough stems.

Stir the parsley, cheese, hazelnuts, and caraway into the rice mixture and taste for salt and pepper.

Preheat the oven to 350°F (180°C).

Place a cabbage leave in front of you and add a generous scoop of the rice filling in the middle, just above where you cut out the stem. Fold the sides inward and roll up the leaf from the unfolded edge to create a small package. Secure with a toothpick and place seam side down in a baking dish. Repeat with the remaining cabbage and filling. Pour the remaining stock over the rolls and cover with aluminum foil.

Bake for 15 minutes. Drizzle some oil over the dish and serve with a side of vegetable puree.

serves 4

Splash of olive oil, plus extra

1 onion, diced

1 big clove garlic, minced

Generous ½ cup (100 g) brown rice

½ cup (100 g) green lentils, ideally Du Puy

2 cups plus 2 tablespoons (500 ml) vegetable stock

8 to 12 leaves Savoy cabbage

Sea salt

1 bunch fresh parsley, finely chopped

⅔ cup (100 g) crumbled feta cheese

Generous ⅓ cup (50 g) hazelnuts, toasted and chopped

2 teaspoons caraway seeds

Freshly ground black pepper

→→→ A TOUCH OF SUMMER IN YOUR PANTRY ←←←

LASAGNA:
COOK THE SHEETS
FOR 1 MINUTE.

SAUSAGES
FROM THE
FREEZER &
LEFTOVER
SPINACH

COOK WITH
ONION & GARLIC
& SOME PASTA
LIQUID

CAN 'O' TOMATOES
T. PASTE & WINE
FROM WHICH
YOU SWIFTLY
WHIP UP A SAUCE.

SAUSAGE
MEAT ON
TOP OF THE
PASTA
SHEETS.

ROLL UP AND
COVER WITH
TOMATO SAUCE
LEFTOVER
CHEESE
ON TOP
AND BAKE AWAY!

For a minute, it looked like spring had arrived, but then temperatures dropped steeply, and it started pouring again. I longed for summer and didn't feel like getting soaked while biking to the store. So I investigated my cupboard instead. It's my favorite thing to do anyway; making *something* out of seemingly *nothing*. I checked my freezer: two fennel sausages. And my fridge: half a bag of spinach and a cheese rind. Together with some finds from my cupboard, these ingredients turned into a fantastic dish. Just like that. On my plate, the sun was shining and I'd managed to stay bone dry.

CUPBOARD CANNELLONI

Preheat the oven to 350°F (180°C).

Slide the lasagna sheets into a pot of boiling water three at a time and cook for 1 minute. Remove the sheets when they're just about soft. Separate and let them dry spread out on a clean dish towel. Reserve the cooking liquid.

Sauté half of the onions and two-thirds of the garlic in some oil and add the sausage meat in pieces. Fry until the meat is cooked through, then spoon in a ladleful of pasta cooking liquid. Add the spinach and cook until the liquid is reduced. Season with red pepper flakes and some salt if needed.

In a saucepan, sauté the remaining onion and garlic in oil until tender. Add the tomato paste and fry. Douse with the wine and tomatoes. Reduce the sauce somewhat and season with red pepper flakes and salt.

Put 1 tablespoon of the sausage-spinach filling on a short end of a lasagna sheet and roll it up. Place in an oiled baking dish. Repeat until everything is used. Pour the sauce on top and sprinkle with the cheese. Bake the cannelloni for 25 minutes.

serves 4

12 sheets lasagna

2 onions, finely chopped

3 cloves garlic, finely chopped

Splash of olive oil

2 links fennel sausage (about 8¾ ounces/240 g), casings removed

8¾ ounces (250 g) spinach (frozen is fine)

Pinch of red pepper flakes

Sea salt

3 tablespoons tomato paste

½ glass red wine

1 (14.5-ounce/411 g) can diced tomatoes

Chunk of cheese for grating (any type that melts will do)

SLICE BEETS
VERY THINLY
WITH A.
MANDOLIN
SLICER

ARRANGE
THEM LIKE A
RO SE
IN AN OVEN
DISH OR PAN.

↓

DOUSE WITH
BUTTER.
SAUCE WITH
THYME,
SHALLOT, , GARLIC
& VERMOUTH

AND COOK AL DENTE
VOILA

I made this dish for my dearest on Valentine's Day. It was more or less by accident, to be honest, which I didn't mention because he was genuinely moved. By now this day is behind us, but without a doubt your sweetheart will have a birthday coming up this year, or maybe you have to make up for something. If so, instead of buying flowers, you could bake a beet rose. At first glance, it kind of resembles carpaccio, but it's more exciting. Because the beets are cooked in butter and red vermouth, they retain that sweetness. As well as their bite, which is remarkable after baking them for such a long time. It does make the dish tastier, however. I served it with a spinach and blue cheese soufflé.

serves 4

1 pound 2 ounces (500 g) trimmed red beets

5 tablespoons (70 g) butter

2 to 3 shallots, finely chopped

2 cloves garlic, finely chopped

2 teaspoons fresh thyme

½ cup (125 ml) red vermouth

Sea salt and freshly ground black pepper

BEET ROSE

Preheat the oven to 400°F (200°C).

Thoroughly rinse the beets, then peel them. Shave with a mandolin into paper-thin slices (about 1.5 mm thick).

Melt the butter in a saucepan and add the shallots, garlic, and thyme. Let the shallots soften over low heat.

Dip a brush into the warm butter and grease a shallow baking dish. (You can also use a cast-iron skillet.) Shingle the beet slices in circles in the dish so they resemble a rose.

Douse the butter in the saucepan with the vermouth, bring to a boil, and add salt and pepper to taste. Pour over the beet slices, covering everything with a thin layer.

Carefully cover the dish with aluminum foil and bake for 45 minutes. Remove the foil and bake for another 30 minutes.

POP.
CHIOGGIA
BEETS, RED
ONION &
GARLIC
IN THE
OVEN.

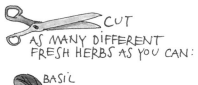

CUT
AS MANY DIFFERENT
FRESH HERBS AS YOU CAN:

BASIL

CILANTRO

CHIVES

MINT

RINSE WATERCRESS

→ TRIM TOUGH
STALKS!

WITH SOME
FETA &
VINAIGRETTE,
YOU'LL BE
GETTING
A TASTY
BITE OF
SPRING.

Of course, I don't know what the situation on your window-sill is right now, but my herb garden is in full festive mood; the chives are about to bug out and the chervil is germinating. Now that I have my own garden, I'm witnessing everything up close. Every hour something wondrous is taking place. I used to be amazed by the wisdom of my friends the two old brothers Georges and Charles, who grew up on a farm in the south of France. They live off the harvest from their garden. They can tell about how the air changes from hour to hour and how this affects their beans, artichokes, or pears. I find these stories fascinating. And now I notice that I'm developing that same awareness. It's addictive. I better watch out, or I'll turn into a farmer in no time. As soon as something comes up in my herb boxes I swoop in; I trim and toss them in my pan to make a colorful roasted vegetable salad, using every windowsill herb I can find.

ROASTED BEET SALAD WITH FRESH SPRING HERBS

Preheat the oven to 350°F (180°C).

Place the beets, onions, and garlic cloves in a baking pan. Drizzle with some oil, sprinkle with salt and pepper, and cover with aluminum foil.

Bake for about 1½ hours, until the beets are al dente, removing the onions and garlic after 1 hour because they're done sooner. Peel everything and cut into wedges.

Make the dressing: Press the garlic into a bowl for the dressing. Whisk in the rest of the ingredients. If it gets too thick, add a few drops of water.

Toss the roasted vegetables with the dressing and then toss with the chopped herbs and watercress. Crumble the feta on top.

serves 4

3 Chioggia beets, trimmed

4 red onions, unpeeled

2 cloves garlic, unpeeled

Splash of olive oil

Sea salt and freshly ground black pepper

A good handful of fresh garden herbs

About 5½ cups (200 g) watercress

3½ ounces (100 g) feta cheese

FOR THE DRESSING

1 tablespoon tahini

1 teaspoon Dijon mustard

Juice of ½ lemon

6 tablespoons (90 ml) sunflower oil

PUREE PAPAYA & GRAPEFRUIT INTO A DIVINE SAUCE

SEASON WITH HONEY! SALT & PEPPER.

AND SERVE WITH A LARGE HALF-GRILLED SALAD:

→ LENTILS!

BUTTERNUT SQUASH ←

SHAVED FENNEL

GRAPEFRUIT

PARSLEY

Leafing through the Mexican cookbook *Hartwood: Bright, Wild Flavors from the Edge of the Yucatán*, I stumbled upon a papaya salad. I'm not much of a papaya fan. Cut in half it looks like an alien has laid eggs inside it, and its flavor is that of bland melon. I mean, just use real melon—it's way more assertive. In the recipe, Chef Eric Werner recommended combining papaya with grapefruit. Because I truly believe in his cooking skills, I decided to make his recipe. I was astonished; that combination gave my salad an earthy perfume that knocked me off my feet. So simple and to the point. From now on I'll know better than to avoid ingredients I don't like; there's always a chance I'll be pleasantly surprised. Cooking is fun, no? Here you'll find my variation on his salad.

serves 4 to 6

1 butternut squash (900 g)

1½ tablespoons smoked paprika

Sea salt and freshly ground black pepper

½ cup (120 ml) olive oil

1 pound 5 ounces (600 g) papaya, peeled and seeded

1 pink grapefruit, halved

Honey

2 cups (400 g) green lentils, preferably Du Puy, cooked

1 fennel bulb, very thinly sliced

Juice from about 1 lime

Generous ¼ cup (15 g) chopped fresh flat-leaf parsley

SMOKY BUTTERNUT SQUASH & PAPAYA SALAD

Preheat the oven to 400°F (200°C).

Cut the squash in half and scrape out the seeds with a spoon. Then cut into slices ⅜ inch (1 cm) thick. Toss these half moons with the paprika, salt and pepper to taste, and ¼ cup (60 ml) of the oil. Spread the squash on a baking sheet and roast for 35 minutes, or until tender.

Puree about half of the papaya together with the juice of ½ grapefruit and a drop of honey. Season with salt and pepper. In a large bowl, combine the lentils with the fennel, lime juice, and the remaining ¼ cup (60 ml) oil. Let stand. Cut the rest of the papaya into cubes.

Separate the grapefruit segments from the membranes with a knife. Do this over the bowl with the lentils so the dripping juice will be mixed in as well. Loosely combine everything: the warm butternut squash, the fruit, lentil mixture, and parsley.

Now spread the pureed papaya onto a large plate. Spoon the salad on top. (You could crumble some feta over it this as well.) Serve immediately.

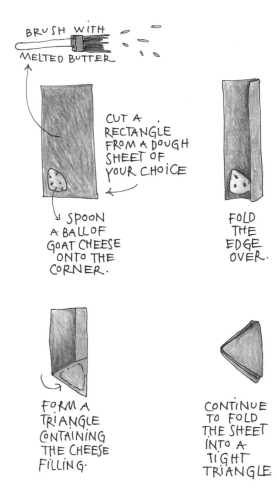

BRUSH WITH
MELTED BUTTER

CUT A
RECTANGLE
FROM A DOUGH
SHEET OF
YOUR CHOICE

SPOON
A BALL OF
GOAT CHEESE
ONTO THE
CORNER.

FOLD
THE
EDGE
OVER.

FORM A
TRIANGLE
CONTAINING
THE CHEESE
FILLING.

CONTINUE
TO FOLD
THE SHEET
INTO A
TIGHT
TRIANGLE.

Outside on the sunny terrace of my neighborhood lunch spot Jaurès in Paris, the half–North African, half-French staff is serving a *chèvre chaud* salad with crispy envelopes of goat cheese folded inside pastry. For a regular *chèvre chaud*, the goat cheese is gratinated on baguette slices, but wrapped in brick dough. It really is pretty delicious. Brick is commonly used for wrapping bites in the Tunisian cuisine. The sheets resemble spring roll pastry or filo dough—and you could use these as well—but they're not quite the same. Brick dough is made from ground cooked semolina; filo dough is made from regular wheat flour. Indonesian wheat spring roll sheets are also made from wheat flour, but these usually have egg white or coconut oil added, rendering them less crispy than filo dough and making them better alternatives for brick pastry. Remember, as with all pastry sheets, carefully cover the ones you're not working with to keep them from drying out. Try different doughs out and decide for yourself which type you prefer.

serves 4

7 ounces (200 g) soft goat cheese

4 to 5 goat-cheese-stuffed Peppadew peppers in oil, finely chopped, or 5 jarred piquillo peppers plus 1 ounce goat cheese

3 tablespoons finely chopped fresh flat-leaf parsley

2 teaspoons spicy mustard

2 tablespoons whiskey or dry sherry

Freshly ground black pepper

5 tablespoons plus 1 teaspoon (75 g) butter, melted

6 sheets filo dough or brick dough, cut in half

FOR THE SALAD

2 tablespoons red wine vinegar

4 to 5 tablespoons (60 to 75 ml) sunflower oil

1 teaspoon spicy mustard

1 clove garlic, finely grated

1 head red oak leaf lettuce

2 to 3 tomatoes, cut into wedges

GOAT CHEESE PASTRY POCKETS

Preheat the oven to 400°F (200°C).

Crumble the goat cheese, combine in a bowl with the Peppadews and parsley, and fold in the mustard and whiskey. Generously season with black pepper.

Brush a strip of dough with the melted butter. Scoop a rounded tablespoonful of the goat cheese mixture onto one end. Fold the opposite edge over, then fold the dough over diagonally. Continue folding over the dough until you have a neatly sealed triangle. Place on a parchment paper–lined baking sheet and repeat with the remaining dough and filling. Bake for 20 minutes, or until nicely crunchy.

Make the salad: Whisk the vinegar, oil, mustard, and garlic together. Toss with the lettuce. Divide the salad among four plates and arrange the tomato wedges on top (and perhaps add some pieces of crisp bacon, nuts, and thin shallot rings—always lovely.) Place three brick bites on each salad and serve.

GROUND ELDER

GARDENER'S
WOE
&
CHEF'S
JOY!

FINELY CHOP
& FRY THE LEAVES
AS YOU WOULD
WITH SPINACH.

WITH
A SHALLOT
& PRESSED

GARLIC

&

A SPLASH
OF OLIVE OIL
IT'S FINGERLICKING
GOOD ON YOUR
PIZZA!

While the rest of the world was foraging for their wild garlic pesto and nettle soup, I was pulling weeds in my garden. Back in the day, my sister and I would earn some pocket money by removing ground elder, also commonly called "gardener's woe." Ground elder is a persistent plant that is almost impossible to get rid of; each chopped-off piece of root continues to grow. But don't worry; this weed is edible. Prepare ground elder like you would spinach, or dry bunches of it upside down in your pantry and crumble a leaf over a soup; it tastes like parsley. Just like that, you turn a problem into a pearl. And after an afternoon of pulling weeds, a weed pizza is very welcome. Trust me.

WHOLE-WHEAT PIZZA WITH GARDENER'S WOE

Make the pizza dough: Combine all the ingredients and knead for 10 minutes. Allow to rise in a warm spot for 1 hour. (This is a good time to pick the ground elder.)

Preheat the oven to as hot as possible, preferably to 500°F (250°C).

Wash the ground elder, remove the stems, and shake dry somewhat. Heat some oil in a large skillet. Sauté the shallot and add the garlic. Chop the ground elder leaves and stir into the shallot and garlic. Continue cooking until tender, and season with salt and red pepper flakes. Set aside.

Roll out the dough into a thin round and place on an oiled (and semolina-dusted, if possible) baking sheet. Top with tomato sauce, the sautéed ground elder, and a sprinkle of a cheese of your choice. Sprinkle with oil and bake in the scorching-hot oven for 10 minutes, or until done.

Never before have weeds tasted this great.

serves 4

FOR THE PIZZA DOUGH

2⅓ cups (300 g) whole-wheat flour

1½ teaspoons instant yeast

1 tablespoon olive oil

½ cup (50 g) grated Parmesan cheese

Pinch of sea salt

Scant ⅔ cup (160 ml) lukewarm water

ON TOP

A good handful of ground elder or spinach (say, 6¼ ounces/175 g)

Splash of olive oil

1 shallot, finely chopped

2 cloves garlic, chopped

Sea salt

Pinch of red pepper flakes

Pinch of semolina (optional)

(Homemade!) tomato sauce

Several types of cheese, of your own preference

RECIPE
WITHOUT A
RECIPE

PLACE A PAN
OF VEGETABLE
BROTH & PEARL
BARLEY IN THE
→OVEN←

GO SIT IN THE
GARDEN.

10 MINS. BEFORE
THE BARLEY IS DONE,
ADD AS MANY GREEN
VEGETABLES AS YOU
CAN FIND. ←

SERVE WITH SOME
CRUMBLED FETA
ON TOP & A SPLASH
OF DELICIOUS OIL.

After a long journey through Japan, I returned home with a craving for vegetables. I had never eaten as well as I did over there, but finding a hearty bowl of fresh veggies took some effort in the land of the rising sun. Back home, my vegetable garden had started growing without me and the shelves in the produce store were brimming with delicate Dutch spring greens. I went to my local park to forage some more, and while I was basking in the warm sun, my oven was baking a nourishing soup that brought tears of joy to my eyes. Actually, this is a recipe sans recipe. I use pearl barley as a base, because it's so nutritious and retains its bite for a long time. Feel free to use whatever you like—farro, orzo, brown rice, or whole wheat grains; pasta is tasty too. But be sure to adjust the cooking time if you do. To prevent having to turn on the oven only for a pot of soup, I made something else with the rest of the vegetables (see the next recipe).

makes 1 pot of soup

6½ cups (1½ L) vegetable stock

1 cup (200 g) pearl barley (preferably presoaked)

Lots of fast-cooking vegetables, such as:

> Generous 1¼ pounds (600 g) unshelled fresh podded peas, or 1¼ cups (200 g) shelled ones

> 1 heaping cup (125 g) haricots verts or green beans, cut into short pieces

> ¾ cup (100 g) green asparagus tips

> 4 scallions, chopped

Handful of (wild) spinach

Freshly ground black pepper

Handful of foraged or garden herbs like wild garlic, parsley, fennel fronds, chives, sprouts, horseradish leaves, bitter cress, French sorrel, edible flowers, basil, and so on

⅔ cup (100 g) crumbled feta cheese

Splash of delicious oil, such as pumpkin seed oil or a peppery olive oil

VEGETABLE SOUP WiTH PEARL BARLEY

Preheat the oven to 400°F (200°C).

Pour the stock into a heavy pan, add the barley, cover, and place in the oven. Set your timer for 35 minutes and go play outside.

Taste whether the barley is almost done or needs a couple more minutes. Presoaked barley could be tender by now, unsoaked barley takes longer; almost 1 hour.

Now add all of the vegetables, except for the herbs. Generously grind black pepper on top.

Place the pan back into the oven for 8 to 10 more minutes, until everything is al dente. Stir in the herbs and spoon into large bowls. Sprinkle with some feta and a splash of oil.

MAKING YOUR OWN 'kind of' RICOTTA

BRING 1 QUART (1 L.) OF MILK
AND THE JUICE OF 1 LEMON
TO A BOIL AND LET SIMMER
UNTIL THE MILK CURDLES.

STRAIN THROUGH
A CHEESECLOTH
PLACED OVER
A SIEVE.

→ LET DRAIN BRIEFLY ←

TURN ONTO A PLATE AND...
VOILA! HOME MADE!
(USE THE WHEY YOU SAVED
FOR BAKING SODA BREAD!)

Ricotta is a wonderful ingredient. It fits really well in these times of trying to throw out as little as possible and reuse everything. The literal meaning of the word *ricotta* is "cooked again"; it's made from the whey that is leftover after making cheese. This can come from cow, goat, sheep, or buffalo milk cheeses. And believe me, after making cheese, producers are left with liters of this light yellow, mildly sour liquid. It's often used as pig feed. However, whey also contains proteins that will solidify once you reheat them—and you get the crumbly by-product called ricotta. Strictly speaking, ricotta can't be called a cheese, but "protein-rich by-product" doesn't sound particularly appealing, does it? Whatever it may be, I stirred heaps of ricotta in with the remaining vegetables from the Vegetable Soup with Pearl Barley (page 47), so I suppose you could say this pie is itself a by-product—and a delicious one at that!

serves 4 for dinner, or 6 for lunch

10 cups (300 g) wild spinach

1 heaping cup (125 g) haricots verts or green beans, cut into short pieces

3 cups plus 2 tablespoons (750 ml) ricotta

3 eggs

3 egg yolks

1½ cups (150 g) grated Parmesan cheese

Freshly ground black pepper

4 scallions, sliced

Handful of foraged or garden herbs like wild garlic or chives, French sorrel, baby dandelion leaves, dill, basil, parsley, and so on

THE GREENEST CRUSTLESS PIE

Preheat the oven to 400°F (200°C).

Thoroughly grease a small springform pan (8½ or 9 inches/ 22 cm).

Blanch the spinach in a saucepan of boiling water, scoop from the pan, and then cook the green beans until al dente; rinse with cold water. Press all the remaining water from the spinach and finely chop.

In a bowl, beat the ricotta, whole eggs, egg yolks, Parmesan, and lots of pepper until smooth. With a spoon, fold in all of the vegetables, including the scallions, and herbs and pour the mixture into the springform pan.

Bake for about 1 hour (depending on the size and depth of your pie). Check now and then; if it feels firm and the middle has become nicely dry, the pie is done.

Let cool slightly and serve with a salad.

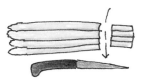

TRIM ENDS FROM
PEELED ASPARAGUS
FOR THE SAUCE.

BLEND
INTO A
SAUCE WITH
CASHEWS &
LEMON JUICE.

ADD
MORE
LEMON JUICE
& ZEST FOR
A HINT
OF TARTNESS

& REDUCE
SLIGHTLY

I've been under the spell of cashews for a while now. In vegan cooking, they are often used as a cream substitute. Without realizing it you'll be eating a nut-based cream sauce that can compete with any crème fraîche–based version. What's more, the cashews only enhance the scrumptiousness; that mild, nutty flavor is a welcome companion to the asparagus and it really complements this dish—tempting us to lick our plates. In the *New York Times*, I saw an amazing method for cooking your asparagus: place them upright in the oven. They maintain more of their flavor and bite that way. Here's my version, which is not quite completely vegan, by the way. If that is important to you, replace the anchovies with sea salt to taste.

serves 4 as part of a dinner, or 6 for lunch

2 pounds 3 ounces (1 kg) asparagus, peeled, bottoms trimmed

2 tablespoons olive oil

Sea salt and freshly ground black pepper

1½ cups (175 g) raw, unsalted cashews, soaked in water for 1 hour

Juice and grated zest of 1 lemon

FOR THE PANGRATATTO

2 dry slices white bread

2 tablespoons raw cashews, coarsely chopped

2 tablespoons olive oil

2 anchovy fillets, chopped

Pinch of chile flakes, to taste

OVEN ASPARAGUS WiTH CASHEW CREAM

Preheat the oven to 400°F (200°C).

Trim one-quarter from the bottom of the asparagus spears and keep for later use. Place the bundle of asparagus upright on a double sheet of aluminum foil on a baking sheet and wrap the foil around it, propping your spears so they remain standing. Sprinkle with oil, salt, and pepper. Wrap in more foil so the spears are fully covered and bake, standing up, for 25 to 35 minutes (depending on thickness), until al dente.

Process the nuts along with 2 cups plus 2 tablespoons (500 ml) water and the asparagus ends to a smooth sauce in a blender. Transfer to a saucepan and bring to a boil. Let simmer for 10 minutes and season with lemon juice/zest, salt, and pepper.

Make the pangratatto: Grind or chop the bread and nuts into a crumb. In a skillet, heat the oil, add the anchovies, and let dissolve. Add the bread-nut crumb and the chile flakes. Cook while stirring until golden brown and crispy.

Pour the cooking liquid from the asparagus into the cashew sauce. Serve the asparagus on a preheated dish, drizzled with cashew cream and sprinkled with the pangratatto.

LEEK...

GARLIC,

SPINAAAACH!,

CHICKPEAS,

&EGG ...YES, PLEASE...

CHEESE:

CALLING ALL
VEGETABLES!
OFF YOU GO
INTO MY FILO
P I E.

♥

— the end —

I spent some time in Ireland. The Irish are fine cooks, especially now that they're beginning to discover the many wonderful ingredients their country produces. But because we were working in a tiny mountain village (often with our dog in tow) and most days we wouldn't sit down for dinner until late, we had to resort to pub grub, invariably from the same establishment. Often bar food implies a lack of vegetables. Or boring ones. In England, I've been in the same situation—to the extent that after fourteen days I was so starved for greens that I decided to prepare them myself on a Primus stove next to my car. It's said that the average Dutch person doesn't meet the recommended dose of 7 ounces (200 grams) per day (it's only 7 ounces, people!), but the British in rural villages sometimes don't even reach a quarter of that. Anyway, I'm home now and I'll be eating only vegetables for the coming weeks, starting with this dish.

VEGGIE FILO PIE

Preheat the oven to 400°F (200°C).

Heat some oil in a wide saucepan and sauté the leeks and garlic for 6 minutes, or until tender. Add the spinach and cook for 5 minutes while stirring. Drain the vegetables in a sieve and use a spoon to press out all liquid. Spoon in the chickpeas.

Beat the egg with the ricotta and season with nutmeg, paprika, salt, and chile flakes. Crumble the feta over the mixture and combine with the vegetables.

Grease an 8-inch (20 cm) springform pan. Line with the sheets of filo dough. Rotate each sheet 90 degrees and let them hang over the edges of the pan. Fill with the ricotta mixture and fold over the hanging dough sheets, making the pie look rustic.

Bake for almost 1 hour, or until the pie is golden brown and done. Serve warm, or cold with a salad.

serves 4

Splash of olive oil

2 leeks, sliced

2 cloves garlic, finely chopped

10½ ounces (300 g) spinach

1 (14-ounce/400 g) can chickpeas, rinsed and drained

1 egg

1 generous cup (250 ml) ricotta, drained

½ teaspoon freshly grated nutmeg

½ teaspoon smoked paprika

Sea salt

Chile flakes

⅔ cup (100 g) crumbled feta cheese

4 to 5 sheets filo dough

THE SUCCESS
OF THIS TART
RELIES ON
PATIENCE.
MAKE A
LITTLE EFFORT
AND YOU'LL
BE SURPRISED!

CUT ALL VEGETABLES AS
THINLY AS POSSIBLE.

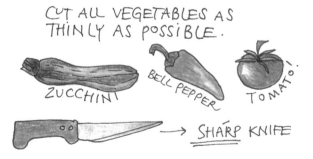

ZUCCHINI   BELL PEPPER   TOMATO!

→ <u>SHARP</u> KNIFE

Done. The vacation is planned and booked. Each year I'm always surprised and realize I should've done all of this by last November because all the cute summer homes are rented. Oh, well. Our first stop will be in Provence, a tradition for us, where my friend Valerie will be awaiting our arrival for afternoon drinks (the *apéro*) with a table filled with rosé, beer, *vin de noix*, pastis, pitchers of water, and buckets of ice cubes. As per tradition she will also serve a home-baked tomato tart. I make the same tart, but use multiple vegetables instead. Tomatoes are often juicy, which isn't conducive to a crunchy crust. The result is gorgeous, as long as you arrange the razor-thin vegetable slices, alternating between the three types, inside the crust's frame with Zen-like dedication. Vacation on a baking sheet: *Santé*.

TARTE AUX LÉGUMES

Preheat the oven to 400°F (200°C).

Place the dough sheet on a parchment paper–lined baking sheet. Using the back of a knife, carve a border about 1 inch (2.5 cm) wide along the edges, creating a frame. Brush with beaten egg. Using a fork, poke holes into the crust inside the frame. Prebake for 12 minutes.

Meanwhile, slice all of the vegetables, using a sharp knife or a mandolin slicer, as thinly as you dare.

Remove the prebaked crust from the oven. If necessary, flatten any air bubbles with the back of a spoon. Fill the crust inside the frame by shingling the various vegetables: slice of zucchini, ring of sweet pepper, tomato, zucchini, and so on. The more meticulous, the nicer the result.

Sprinkle with salt and pepper, a splash of oil, the thyme, and cheese. Bake the tart for 30 minutes. Serve warm or cold.

serves 4

1 (10½-ounce/300 g) package puff pastry, rolled out into a rectangle

1 egg, beaten

1½ zucchinis

4 orange sweet pointed peppers, or 1 large orange or yellow bell pepper

5 to 6 tomatoes

Sea salt and freshly ground black pepper

Splash of olive oil

2 teaspoons fresh thyme leaves

6 tablespoons (35 g) grated Parmesan cheese

BEETS &
RHU-
BARB: MATCH MADE
IN HEAVEN ♡

ROAST IN THE OVEN.
ADD:

PARSLEY & TARRAGON

BABY SPINACH →

CHUNK
OF FETA

LEMON & OLIVE OIL

After St. John's Day on June 24 (or after June 21, the longest day of the year), white asparagus and rhubarb are no longer harvested. Our seasons are related to the position of the Earth relative to the sun, and after June 21 the Northern Hemisphere is turning farther away from the sun—the so-called summer solstice (our winter solstice is on December 21). This shift has an effect on nature. After the summer solstice, many plants develop flowers and young sprouts, or they grow out.

Therefore, rhubarb and asparagus plants are no longer harvested, allowing them to grow new sprouts to store energy for the coming year undisturbed. Another reason is that closer to June 21, rhubarb leaves produce more oxalic acid, which negatively affects their flavor. So the third week of June is typically the last opportunity to buy rhubarb and white asparagus. Make the most of it. You'll have to wait a long time until the next harvest.

serves 4

1 pound 10 ounces (750 g) red beets

10½ ounces (300 g) rhubarb, cut into 1-inch (2.5 cm) pieces

4 tablespoons (50 g) sugar

Large bunch fresh flat-leaf parsley (1 ounce/30 g), coarsely chopped

¼ cup (10 g) tarragon or dill, chopped

5¼ ounces (150 g) baby spinach

1 cup (150 g) crumbled feta cheese

4 tablespoons (60 ml) olive oil

Splash of fresh lemon juice

Sea salt and freshly ground black pepper

RHUBARB BEET SALAD

Preheat the oven to 400°F (200°C).

Place all of the beets in a baking dish, cover with aluminum foil, and bake for 40 to 50 minutes, until tender. Combine the rhubarb with the sugar and place them in the baking dish with the beets for the final 12 minutes.

Let the beets cool somewhat, then rub off the skins. Break into pieces. Drain the rhubarb over a bowl, saving the liquid.

In a large serving bowl, gently combine the rhubarb with the beets, parsley, tarragon, spinach, and cheese.

Whisk together a dressing from the rhubarb juice and the oil, seasoning with lemon juice, salt, and pepper. Sprinkle onto the salad and serve.

MIX LUKEWARM
WHITE WINE &
YEAST (INSTANT!)
& LET STAND FOR
A LITTLE WHILE.

USING A WHISK,
COMBINE PIZZA
FLOUR (TYPO OO) &
SEMOLINA &
SALT.

ADD THE YEAST
MIXTURE, MORE
WINE & OLIVE
OIL AND KNEAD
THOROUGHLY.

LET THE DOUGH
RISE, TOP WITH
MY CRUSHED
TOMATO SAUCE
& BAKE TO A
PERFECT CRISP
IN A PIPING HOT
O V E N!

Regular all-purpose flour has an average extraction rate and ash content (in France it's called type 55), making it especially useful for common baked goods that require some level of leavening such as pancakes, pound cakes and bread, or cookies. For *truly* good bread you want a higher extraction rate (type 65), which has better leavening properties. This type of flour is often used in bread mixes, and you can buy it at a specialty store or directly from a mill. All-purpose flour (type 45) is a finer version of wheat flour and it contains more gluten, making it even more suited for baking cakes and pastries. Italians use a different scale. Their tipo 00 compares to the French type 40, a very fine hard wheat flour that is used for things that hardly need to rise, if at all, such as pasta. For making pizza or focaccia, there's farina pizza tipo 00—a flour mixture. When making focaccia I add some extra hard semolina flour to help the leavening and provide that necessary gluten. By substituting white wine for water you emulate the hint of sourness that makes sourdough bread so lovely.

serves 4 to 6 as a snack or side dish

2½ teaspoons (8 g) instant yeast

About 1 cup plus 2 tablespoons (275 ml) lukewarm white wine, plus a dash extra

3 cups plus 2 tablespoons (400 g) farina pizza tipo 00 or all-purpose flour

½ cup plus 1 tablespoon (100 g) semolina

1 teaspoon (5 g) sea salt, plus extra for the sauce

3 tablespoons plus 1 teaspoon (50 ml) olive oil, plus extra

1 pound 2 ounces (500 g) mini plum tomatoes or cherry tomatoes

4 cloves garlic, finely chopped

Leaves from a few sprigs fresh oregano

Freshly ground black pepper

FOCACCIA WITH CRUSHED TOMATOES

Mix the yeast with a splash of wine and let stand for 5 minutes. Combine the flours and the salt. Form an indentation in the middle and while stirring, pour in the dissolved yeast, the remaining wine, and the oil. Continue to knead well. Focaccia dough should be nice and smooth but not too sticky. Add more flour or wine if needed. Cover and let rise for 1 hour.

Preheat the oven to 425°F (220°C); if you want you can place a pizza stone in the oven.

Heat some oil in a saucepan. Crush the tomatoes with your hands and cook them. Add the garlic, oregano, and salt and pepper and reduce to a thick sauce. Let cool.

Press out the dough and roll out into a rectangle. Using your fingertips, press dimples into the dough. Spread the sauce over the dough and generously sprinkle with a half-wine, half-water mixture. Bake for about 20 minutes, until golden.

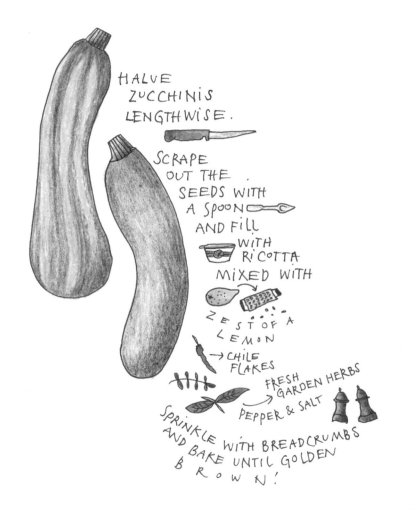

HALVE
ZUCCHINIS
LENGTHWISE.

SCRAPE
OUT THE
SEEDS WITH
A SPOON
AND FILL
WITH
RICOTTA
MIXED WITH

ZEST OF A
LEMON

→ CHILE
FLAKES

FRESH
GARDEN HERBS
PEPPER & SALT

SPRINKLE WITH BREADCRUMBS
AND BAKE UNTIL GOLDEN
B R O W N !

The French name for zucchini, *courgette*, comes from the word *courge*, meaning "squash." So *courgette* is a diminutive and it refers to summer squash, which we eat unpeeled, rind and all. It's a smaller variety of the squashes and pumpkins we harvest in the fall. And just like there are many types of squash, there also are many types of *courgette*. At my neighborhood store I increasingly spot yellow ones. These taste different from the green ones; yellow squash are more pronounced. And because their pulp is a little firmer, they maintain their shape better when baked or grilled than their more watery—but nonetheless tasty—green cousins. I grow green and striped zucchini in my garden. If you grow your own zucchini you have the luxury of deciding exactly when you want to harvest them; small ones, raw and thinly sliced, are really delicious in a salad. The really large ones are great for making soup, but the medium-sized ones—I harvest them when they're still slightly smaller than those sold at the average store—are great for baking. The following recipe, for instance, is a wonderfully fresh late-summer dish.

serves 4

4 zucchini

Scant 1½ cups (350 ml) ricotta

Grated zest of 1 lemon

1 teaspoon chile flakes, or to taste

Small handful of garden herbs, finely chopped

Sea salt and freshly ground black pepper

Panko or homemade breadcrumbs

ZUCCHINI WITH RICOTTA & LEMON

Preheat the oven to 400°F (200°C).

Halve the zucchini lengthwise and scoop out the seeds with a spoon. Place on a parchment paper–lined baking sheet.

In a bowl, combine the ricotta, lemon zest, chile flakes, and herbs and fill the hollow zucchini with this mixture. Sprinkle with salt and pepper and breadcrumbs.

Bake the zucchini halves for 35 minutes, until tender through and through. Serve as a side dish with chicken or fish or as a vegetarian main course along with some other vegetables or a salad.

CUBE 1 CELERIAC
BAKE WITH
GARLIC &
COOK IN MILK

ARRANGE QUARTERED
BEETS AND ONION
ON A BAKING SHEET.
BAKE AL DENTE.

PUREE
IN
THE
BLENDER

WHIP UP A
VINAIGRETTE

FROM BALSAMIC
VINEGAR, HONEY,
THYME, TARRAGON
& OLIVE OIL

SERVE
THE BALSAMIC
BEETS ON TOP OF
THE CELERIAC CREAM.
HOW GOOD IS THAT?

Beets. I can't get enough of them. I sowed them in my vegetable garden. Not too many, just for fun. Two rows of yellow ones because they are so deliciously sweet. Two rows of Chioggia, the red-and-white-striped ones, because they're so beautiful. And just a short row of red beets, because the supermarket has those too. Mine didn't grow as big as the specimens I buy, but wow, what flavor! Those tiny sweet beets, straight from my planters, turned out to be the tastiest ingredient my garden produced this year. Next year I'll sow three times as many.

BALSAMIC BEETS WITH A CELERIAC CREAM

Preheat the oven to 400°F (200°C).

Spread the quartered beets and onion on a baking sheet. Sprinkle with 2 tablespoons of the oil and a pinch of salt and pepper. Slide into the middle of the oven and bake until al dente, about 35 minutes.

In a bowl, stir the vinegar and honey together and add the remaining 1 tablespoon oil. Add three-quarters of the herbs and a pinch of salt and pepper. Douse the tray of beets and onions with the balsamic vinaigrette.

Make the celeriac cream: Briefly fry the garlic in the olive oil. Add the celeriac and stir. Douse with the milk and a glass of water if necessary to cover. Add salt and pepper to taste. Cover with a lid and simmer for 20 minutes, or until the celeriac is tender. Pulse everything in a blender to a smooth puree and season with salt and pepper.

Spoon into four bowls. Scoop the beets and onions on top. Sprinkle with the remaining herbs and serve.

serves 4 as a side dish,
or 2 as a main course

4 to 5 beets, peeled and quartered

2 red onions, peeled and quartered

3 tablespoons olive oil

Sea salt and freshly ground black pepper

2 tablespoons balsamic vinegar

½ tablespoon honey

1 tablespoon fresh thyme leaves

1 tablespoon finely chopped fresh tarragon

FOR THE CELERIAC CREAM

3 cloves garlic, pressed

1 tablespoon olive oil

1 celery root, peeled and cut into ½-inch (12 mm) cubes

1⅔ cups (400 ml) milk

Sea salt and freshly ground black pepper

SLICE
ONIONS!

AND SAUTÉ
UNTIL SOFT.

CUT SCALLION

CUT CHIVES

GRATE
CHEESE

→ CHEESE
→ ONIONS
→ CHEESE
→ ONIONS

LAYER EVERYTHING
IN A BAKING PAN
LINED WITH
SOFT DOUGH →
COVER WITH
DOUGH
AND
BAKE
♥

Did you know that the Netherlands is the world's largest exporter of onions? Many of these head to Africa, where onions are very popular. However, in recent years African onion production has soared, lowering the demand for the Dutch onion. As a result, the Netherlands is now sitting on a giant surplus. We made a television episode about it, and guess what? After filming, I was left with an onion surplus of my own. That very night I made this English onion pie with it. Onion is delicious, versatile, and cheap. Why not eat it more often?

CHEESE ONION PIE

Start the filling: Melt the butter in a heavy pan and fry the onions until translucent and soft, about 10 minutes. Douse with about 7 tablespoons (100 ml) water. Cook to reduce until most of the water has evaporated and season with salt and pepper. Set aside.

Make the dough: In a pan, melt the butter for the dough together with a scant ½ cup (110 ml) water. Combine the flour and salt and pour in the warm butter mixture. Stir to make a cohesive dough.

Preheat the oven to 350°F (180°C). Grease a springform pan (about 9½ inches/24 cm).

Roll out two-thirds of the dough into a large round that more than covers the bottom of the baking pan. Don't worry if the slab tears, you can easily press the pieces back together.

Combine the cheese with the chives and scallions. Spread half of the fried onions over the dough bottom, then add half of the cheese. Repeat: spread the remaining half of the onions on top of that, and sprinkle the remaining cheese on top. Roll out the rest of the dough and place on top. Using a fork, seal the edges and poke some holes to allow the steam to escape.

Bake for 45 minutes, or until nicely golden brown. Let the pie cool a little before cutting it.

serves 4

FOR THE FILLING

1 tablespoon plus 2 teaspoons (25 g) butter

6 onions, cut into thin rings

Sea salt and freshly ground black pepper

4⅓ cups (500 g) shredded cheddar or another aged cheese

1 bunch fresh chives, finely chopped

4 scallions, finely chopped

FOR THE DOUGH

10½ tablespoons (150 g) butter

3 cups plus 2 tablespoons (400 g) all-purpose flour

½ teaspoon salt

1 egg, beaten

WRAP BEETS
IN FOIL

BAKE FOR ±45 MINS.
IN A HOT
OVEN.

GENTLY
CRUSH THEM.

AND FRY THEM!

VOILA:
FRIED BEETSTEAK!

We've been eating a lot less meat at home, just like a lot of people around me. I've noticed that many of them have their doubts about "meat substitutes," though. The thing is, there really is no need to fill a gap between the vegetables and potatoes on your plate. You simply prepare a dish that happens to not contain meat—that's something else altogether. Of course, you can fry an egg or make something out of vegan meat (I still wonder what that might be), but don't worry that I'm about to try to sell you on some sort of bland tofu burger. No way, I won't do it. There's so much more inspiration to be found from honest vegetables. Beetsteak, for instance: a lovely little dish, super easy. More so than actual steak, which is easy to ruin. Not beetsteak. Success every time. Serve your beetsteaks on a chunky tabouleh with lots of chickpeas. Pretty tasty.

serves 4

6 beets

2 tablespoons grapefruit juice or orange juice

1 tablespoon red wine vinegar

4 tablespoons (60 ml) olive oil

Sea salt and freshly ground black pepper

2 tablespoons minced fresh mint leaves

2 tablespoons minced fresh chives

6 tablespoons (60 ml) plain Greek yogurt

BAKED BEETSTEAK

Preheat the oven to 400°F (200°C).

Wrap all of the beets in aluminum foil. Place them in a baking dish and bake for 40 to 50 minutes, or until tender.

Let cool somewhat and rub off the skins. Use your palm to gently push down on the beets. Not so hard that you crush them but just enough to flatten them a bit.

In a wide bowl, whisk together the grapefruit juice, vinegar, 2 tablespoons of the oil, salt and pepper to taste, and half of the herbs. Roll the beets through this mixture. Let stand for 30 minutes.

In a skillet, heat the remaining 2 tablespoons oil over medium heat. Fry the beets for 5 minutes on each side, or until they start to brown.

Stir the remaining marinade into the yogurt, spoon over the fried beetsteaks, and serve.

BAKE YOUR SWEET POTATOES

AND HALF THEM

SCOOP OUT THE INSIDES

FILL WITH:

SPINACH, AGED CHEESE,

PAP PAPRIKAPOWDER → CAYENNE → SALT & PEPPER.

ALL OF THIS MIXED WITH THE BAKED POTATO.

BAKE BRIEFLY

AND SERVE WITH SOUR CREAM & CILANTRO ON TOP.

Whenever I mention sweet potatoes, the husband immediately pulls a long face. He finds them mushy and bland, kind of like baby food. I can see his point. When low-carb recipes call for sweet potato oven fries I always feel duped; not only do they not taste like potato, they really never turn out crispy. That's because sweet potatoes aren't potatoes. They're a root vegetable originally from South America. But because they grow underground and look like potatoes, they nearly share the same name. It would be better to rename them completely. Change those expectations, because although the *batata*—or yam—is no traditional Dutch vegetable like the potato, it is in fact delicious. Season this dish generously. Who's talking about baby food now?

serves 6 as a side dish, or 3 as a main course (along with a salad, for instance)

3 sweet potatoes of equal size, washed

7 ounces (200 g) spinach

2 tablespoons olive oil

Juice and grated zest of ½ lemon

1 teaspoon paprika

Pinch of ground cayenne

Sea salt and freshly ground black pepper

¾ cup (75 g) grated aged Cheddar cheese

Generous ½ cup (125 ml) sour cream

Handful of chopped fresh cilantro

TWICE-BAKED SWEET POTATOES

Preheat the oven to 400°F (200°C).

Place the sweet potatoes on a parchment paper–lined baking sheet and bake for about 1 hour. Depending on their size they should be nicely baked by then. If you can easily stick in a knife, they're done.

Halve the sweet potatoes and use a spoon to hollow out the middle part, leaving just a thin shell. Set the potato flesh aside.

Cook the spinach in some oil. Douse with lemon juice, then drain and press out as much liquid as possible. Finely chop.

Combine the chopped spinach with the sweet potato flesh and season with lemon zest, paprika, cayenne, and salt and pepper. Stuff the hollowed-out skins with the mixture and put back on the baking sheet. Sprinkle with the cheese.

Return them to the oven for another 10 minutes or so to make sure they're nicely hot and the cheese has melted.

Serve with some sour cream and cilantro on top.

CHOP
SOME CAVOLO NERO
AND SAUTÉ UNTIL.
TENDER IN SOME OLIVE
OIL WITH GARLIC &
A SPLASH OF
WATER.

BEAT EGG
CRÈME FRAÎCHE,
PARMESAN,
HAZELNUTS
AND

RED CHILES
AS MANY AS YOU
CAN HANDLE.

COMBINE WITH
THE KALE
& STUFF THE
MUSHROOMS.

NICELY GRILL PORTOBELLO'S
IN A GRILL PAN.

↠→ BAKE ←↞

My Italian friend Maria is an amazing cook, better than any-one. At least that's the myth she created around herself, and I'm willing to believe her. Maria's parents had an olive grove in Calabria. While folding laundry together Maria tells me stories of how her mother used to make fresh mozzarella and then ricotta from the leftover whey. How the fireplace was always burning so that they could steam beans and that the next morning the glowing embers were used to bake the day's bread. How her family preserved their own summer vegeta-bles for the winter. She goes back often. For instance, when her sister has a pig slaughtered the entire family lends a hand to process the whole animal. Whenever she returns from one of her trips back home she brings me something. Sometimes it's a fragrant orange from her brother's garden, and recently she gave me four Calabrese peppers. They came with a warn-ing: besides being the most delicious peppers ever, they are also dangerously hot. I used a piece of the first chile pepper in the following—faintly Italian—side dish, especially for Maria.

serves 4

4 portobello mushrooms, stems removed

3 cups (200 g) finely chopped cavalo nero (Tuscan kale)

Olive oil

2 cloves garlic, finely chopped

2 eggs, beaten

2 tablespoons crème fraîche

½ cup (50 g) grated Parmesan cheese

2 tablespoons chopped roasted hazelnuts

Pinch of minced red (Calabrian) pepper (or to taste)

Sea salt

STUFFED AUTUMN PORTOBELLOS

Heat a grill pan on the stove. Place the mushroom caps, gills facing up, on top. Leave for about 20 minutes, or until small drops begin to form between the gills. Transfer to a plate and set aside.

Preheat the oven to 350°F (180°C).

Fry the kale in some oil with the garlic until wilted, then transfer to a bowl and stir in the eggs, crème fraîche, cheese, and hazelnuts, and add as much finely chopped Calabrian peppers as you like (and some salt). Generously fill the mush-rooms with the mixture. Place on a baking sheet and bake until just done, about 20 minutes. Serve.

A TOMATILLO IS JUST BEAUUUTIFUL!

↳ PEAL OFF THE HUSKS & RINSE THE STICKY FRUITS.

ROAST WITH 1 FRESH JALAPEÑO

→ or more if you like!

REMOVE STEM

& LOTS OF GARLIC

PUREE IN THE BLENDER, TOGETHER WITH LIME

CILANTRO & SCALLION

Recently we were shooting for our TV show in the Dutch province of Drenthe. It was there, in the wonderful vegetable gardens of farmer André, that I suddenly spotted them: towering plants brimming with tomatillos. How nice! I'd never seen these exotic fruits on a plant before, and here they were, in the Netherlands, of all places. The tomatillo is a fruit that somewhat resembles the Cape gooseberry (they're both called Physalis) and the green tomato. They originally come from Mexico and were important ingredients of the Mayan and Aztec cuisines. They're not always easy to find, but because homemade tomatillo salsa goes so well with tortilla chips or a grilled hen, I happily bike the extra mile to buy them. As should you: this recipe is so incredibly easy that you'd be crazy not to make it. André's tomatillos are sold at the Amsterdam farmers market, but you can also find them at Mexican grocery and produce stores. They're beautiful. And delicious.

makes 1 jar

About 20 small tomatillos
(1 pound 10 ounces/750 g)

1 jalapeño (or more), stemmed

4 cloves garlic, unpeeled

2 to 3 scallions, chopped

1 bunch fresh cilantro (about
¾ ounce/20 g)

Juice of 2 limes

Pinch of sea salt

ROASTED TOMATILLO SALSA

Preheat the broiler to high heat.

Husk the tomatillos and clean the sticky skin by washing them in a large pot of water. Spread out on a parchment paper–lined baking sheet. Add the jalapeño and garlic cloves and broil everything for 14 minutes, or until black marks begin to form. Turn the vegetables over halfway through the baking time.

Meanwhile, process the remaining ingredients to a pulp in a blender. Squeeze the garlic cloves out of their skins and add them to the blender, together with the other contents of the baking sheet, and blend into a thick green sauce. Store the salsa in a clean jar in the fridge, where it will keep for 1 week.

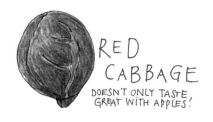

RED CABBAGE

DOESN'T ONLY TASTE
GREAT WITH APPLES!

»»→ CAN ALSO BE PREPARED IN THE OVEN ←«

QUARTER

SPRINKLE
WITH GARLIC,
CHEESE & CRUMBS

ROAST &
TOSS WITH
THE BEST
BALSAMIC
YOU HAVE.

Red cabbage is also known as purple cabbage. The red-purple color of the leaves is caused by the plant's pigments, which turn either more red, or purple, depending on the pH level of the soil. So the location of a cabbage plant determines its color. In order to retain the nice red tint while cooking them, you can add a splash of acid; my mother used ketchup (for the sweet-sour effect), but a splash of vinegar (and some sugar) works as well. Otherwise the cabbage will turn blue when cooked. I, on the other hand, simply toss the cabbage wedges into the oven. They retain their beautiful deep purple hue while becoming crispy on the outside and staying juicy within. Such an autumn treat. You can serve them with delicious mashed celeriac or mashed sweet potato and cavolo nero with roasted garlic.

serves 4

4 tablespoons (55 g) butter, melted

3 cloves garlic, very finely chopped

Generous ¾ cup (75 g) grated Parmesan cheese

4 tablespoons panko or homemade breadcrumbs

½ red cabbage, cut into 6 wedges, with the stem on

Maldon sea salt flakes and freshly ground black pepper

A few drops of good balsamic vinegar

RED CABBAGE WiTH PARMESAN & GARLiC

Preheat the oven to 400°F (200°C).

Brush a baking sheet with some melted butter.

In a bowl, combine the rest of the butter with the garlic, cheese, and breadcrumbs.

Place the cabbage wedges, spaced a little apart, on the baking sheet. Divide the butter and cheese mixture among the cabbage wedges and spread evenly. Season with salt flakes and pepper if desired.

Bake the wedges for 30 minutes, or until the tops are crispy and it's easy to stick a knife into them.

Sprinkle with some vinegar and serve.

KNOW YOUR ROOTS

WHAT IS THE WHAT
IN THIS FAMILY

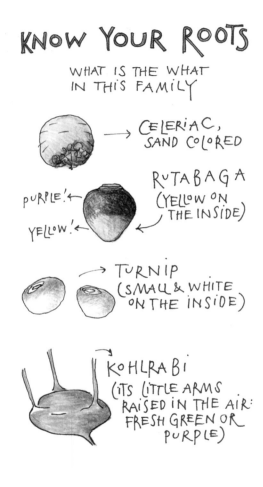

→ CELERIAC,
SAND COLORED

RUTABAGA
(YELLOW ON
THE INSIDE)

PURPLE!←

YELLOW!←

→ TURNIP
(SMALL & WHITE
ON THE INSIDE)

KOHLRABI
(ITS LITTLE ARMS
RAISED IN THE AIR:
FRESH GREEN OR
PURPLE)

Kohlrabi is one of those vegetables that is easily overlooked. Not to be confused with rutabaga, kohlrabi (or German turnip) looks like a root vegetable sticking its arms up in the air. They're mostly light green but can also be purple. They're really delicious. Peeled and raw in a salad, they taste a little like radish, but you can also quarter them and throw them in a stew. Sliced or cut into chunks, they can be fried. And, of course, you can bake them whole in the oven. Because anything you can do with a beet, you can do with a kohlrabi. The kohlrabi is also the only one out of the common family of tubers that grows aboveground. That's because this tuber is in fact a pantry, where the plant stores its nutrients, making kohlrabi exceptionally healthy to boot. I love it. This recipe is a lovely little vegetarian main course, delicious with a tabouleh of grains and lots of fresh herbs on the side.

serves 4

4 kohlrabi

Splash of olive oil

Sea salt and freshly ground black pepper

1 cup (150 g) crumbled feta cheese

2 roasted sweet pointed red peppers, peeled and seeded

½ to 1 tablespoon pickled jalapeño rings

Some sprigs of fresh flat-leaf parsley, finely chopped

Pinch of chile flakes (or to taste)

KOHLRABI WITH A SPICY CREAM OF POINTED RED PEPPER

Preheat the oven to 400°F (200°C).

Clean the kohlrabi, remove the stems, and brush with some oil. Place on a baking sheet and sprinkle with salt and pepper. Bake for 1½ to 2 hours (depending on their size), until charred on the outside and tender within.

Let cool slightly, then peel. If you'd like, you can slice the kohlrabi before serving.

In a food processor, puree the feta, sweet peppers, jalapeño, and parsley. Spread the red cream onto a large platter. Place the peeled kohlrabi on top. Drizzle with some oil and sprinkle with a pinch of salt and chile flakes if you like, then serve.

HALVE

CARVE SLITS
ALONG THE SIDES

AS WELL
AS THE
TOP

STUD
WITH THIN
SLICES OF
GARLIC

GOOD
QUALITY!

BRUSH WITH
OLIVE OIL

SEASON
& BAKE ➡ YUM.

Recently I visited the region of Apulia, in the heel of the Italian boot. In nearly every restaurant they served an antipasto of a halved grilled eggplant, with or without a topping. Each time it was cooked to perfection: Not too long, which causes the eggplant to lose its form and makes it more suitable for a baba ghanoush dip; but not too short, either, which would render it hard and bland. No, without exception these eggplants were meaty, with a profound grilled flavor. This is what I love so much; doing just one thing really well and then serving the result as is. Try to follow that approach with this recipe!

serves 4 as an appetizer

2 eggplant

Sea salt and freshly ground
black pepper

Generous splash of peppery
olive oil

2 large cloves garlic, thinly
sliced

1 ball super-fresh burrata
(8¾ ounces/250 g)

Chile flakes and flaky salt
(optional)

GRILLED EGGPLANT WITH BURRATA

Preheat the oven to 435°F (225°C).

Halve the eggplants lengthwise. Carve several deep slits along the sides, as well as the top. Make sure not to cut them all the way through. Lightly sprinkle with salt and pepper. Brush the cut sides and top with oil. Stud the slits with garlic slices.

Place the eggplant halves on a baking sheet in the oven, cut sides up. Bake for 45 minutes, or until they're tender but not quite beginning to fall apart. The top should be nicely browned. Brush with some oil halfway through the cooking time.

After baking, let rest for 10 minutes. Cut the burrata in half. Divide the creamy fresh cheese over the eggplant halves. Drizzle with some really good olive oil. Sprinkle with (chile!) pepper and salt flakes, if you'd like. Serve right away.

Delicious, right? Holy moly. Heavenly.

OOOOH!

OOOY-
STER
MMM-
MUSH-
ROOMS
SO GOOD...

ROL OUT
PIZZA /
FLAMMKUCHEN
DOUGH

TOP WITH

GARLIC,

CRÈME
FRAÎCHE

THYME   SCALLION

CHEESE
& BAKED
OYSTER
MUSHROOMS

⇒ MUSHROOMKUCHEN

The traditional thin-crust pizza from the French Alsace region isn't topped with tomato sauce but with crème fraîche (as well as bacon and onion). While the French call this pizza variety *tarte flambée,* just across the border in Germany it's known as *flammkuchen.* The Italians have their own tomato-free pizza. They replace the crème fraîche with mascarpone, and then top it according to regional taste and call it *pizza bianca* (white pizza). I like to eat my *flammkuchen* topped with a *Bergkäse* like Gruyère or Taleggio and some meaty oyster mushrooms. To each his own, I guess.

MUSHROOM FLAMMKUCHEN

Mix half of the water with the yeast. Let stand for 7 minutes. Combine the flour and the salt in a bowl. Pour in the yeast mixture and add the butter. While stirring, add the rest of the water in splashes until the dough begins to come together. Continue kneading for another 10 minutes.

In a covered and greased bowl, let the dough rise for 1 hour.

Make the topping: Heat a skillet with some oil and fry the mushrooms, garlic, and thyme, stirring until tender. Add three-quarters of the scallions. Season with salt and pepper. Set aside.

Preheat the oven to 425°F (225°C).

Briefly knead the dough some more and divide into two portions. On a lightly floured work surface, roll out one portion of dough as thinly as possible. Transfer the thin dough slab to a sheet of parchment paper on a baking sheet and spread with crème fraîche. Spread half of the mushroom mixture and half of the cheese on top.

Bake for 12 to 15 minutes, until golden brown. Sprinkle with half of the remaining scallions and serve while you make the second one.

makes 2 pizzas

⅔ cup to ¾ cup (175 to 200 ml) lukewarm water

1½ teaspoons instant yeast

2⅓ cups (300 g) all-purpose flour, plus extra for dusting

Pinch of sea salt

2 tablespoons butter, melted

FOR THE TOPPING

3 tablespoons olive oil

1 pound 2 ounces (500 g) oyster mushrooms, shredded

1 clove garlic, finely chopped

Fresh thyme

3 scallions, sliced

Sea salt and freshly ground black pepper

10 tablespoons (150 ml) crème fraîche

7 ounces (200 g) Taleggio cheese (or Gruyere, raclette or mozzarella), cubed

PRECOOK THE
ONIONS →
PREFERABLY
IN BROTH

CRUMBLE
(BLUE) CHEESE
HAVE HEAVY CREAM,
BAY LEAF & BLACK
PEPPER READY,

HALVE
THE COOKED
ONIONS

COMBINE EVERYTHING
IN AN OVEN DISH
AND BROIL
UNTIL GOLDEN !

Oh, the lowly onion. What a modest role it plays in our kitchen. You often forget how divine it is even though so many recipes begin with an onion. Sautéed in butter or oil, they smell like heaven, and only then does the dish really take off. But there's no reason why the onion shouldn't be playing the lead role. This recipe will change the way you look at it. My neighborhood supermarket carries many varieties of onions. The following recipe offers you the opportunity to experiment. I'd urge you to be creative. Try it. We ate this dish in combination with a roasted chicken and a green salad. It was onion-believable.

ONiON WiTH CREAM, SAGE & STiLTON

Bring a saucepan of broth to a boil. Peel the onions but leave them whole and add to the broth. Again bring to a boil and reduce the heat to medium, allowing the onions to cook slowly.

Cook them for 45 minutes to 1 hour, until soft. You should feel no resistance when poking them with a sharp knife. The cooking time depends on the size of the onions.

Meanwhile, preheat the oven to 400°F (200°C).

Scoop the onions from the pan, then halve and place them cut side down in a baking dish. Drizzle with the cream, press sage leaves in between, and crumble the cheese on top. Sprinkle with pepper and bake for 25 minutes, or until golden brown.

serves 4 as a side dish

1 saucepan full of broth (vegetable, beef, or chicken; enough to submerge everything)

4 large onions

¾ cup plus 1 tablespoon (200 ml) heavy cream

6 fresh sage leaves

3½ ounces (100 g) Stilton cheese (or another aged cheese such as Parmesan or Cheddar)

Freshly ground black pepper

 USING A
SHARP KNIFE
CARVE.
AN X INTO
THE BOTTOM
OF EACH
TOMATO

 PLACE THE NAKED
TOMATOES ON A
BAKING SHEET
& DRY THEM IN
A WARM OVEN.

 BRIEFLY
SUBMERGE
THEM INTO
BOILING
WATER &
PEEL OFF
THE SKINS

 MY HUSBAND OOF SERVES
THESE WITH EQUAL PARTS
OF PONZU (OR SOY & LEMON),
OLIVE OIL & SESAME

At home, we regularly eat Japanese food. This isn't so much thanks to me but rather to my husband, Oof Verschuren. He devours every book and movie about Japanese cuisine that comes out and he is without exaggeration one of the best Japanese chefs I know (excluding "real" ones). He doesn't prepare standard sushi, but true homemade Japanese food: dishes whose existence I was completely unaware of and whose names I cannot pronounce. When I asked him for a Japanese oven dish for this book, he could only come up with one. The Japanese aren't big oven chefs. They often cook over open fire, but that isn't quite the same. Therefore, I give you this minimalist recipe inspired by Nobu Matsushisa, a celebrated Japanese chef who became famous for his Japanese-Peruvian fusion cuisine during the '90s. Oof makes these tomatoes nearly every time he cooks for me. They really are incredible flavor bombs that will bring you tears of joy. It is one of my all-time favorite dishes.

serves 4 as a side dish

Handful of mini vine tomatoes

Splash of ponzu

Splash of olive oil

Pinch of roasted sesame seeds (optional)

NOBU'S TOMATOES

Preheat the oven to 210°F (100°C).

Bring a large pot of water to a boil. Using a pointed knife, carve a small x on the bottom of each little tomato, but do make sure to leave the stems on. Carefully let the tomatoes slide into the boiling water, then scoop them out with a slotted spoon after a few seconds. Now you can easily peel off the skin. Leave the stems on.

Place them on a parchment paper–lined baking sheet and dry them in the warm oven for 4 hours. Oof serves them straight after they've cooled off with a drop of ponzu and oil and sometimes a sprinkle of roasted sesame seeds. Nobu lets them dry uncovered in the fridge for another 6 hours. It's a versatile dish that works with everything, from fish and meat to cheese.

VEGETABLE SOUP WITH PEARL BARLEY, PAGE 47

TARTE AUX LÉGUMES, PAGE 55

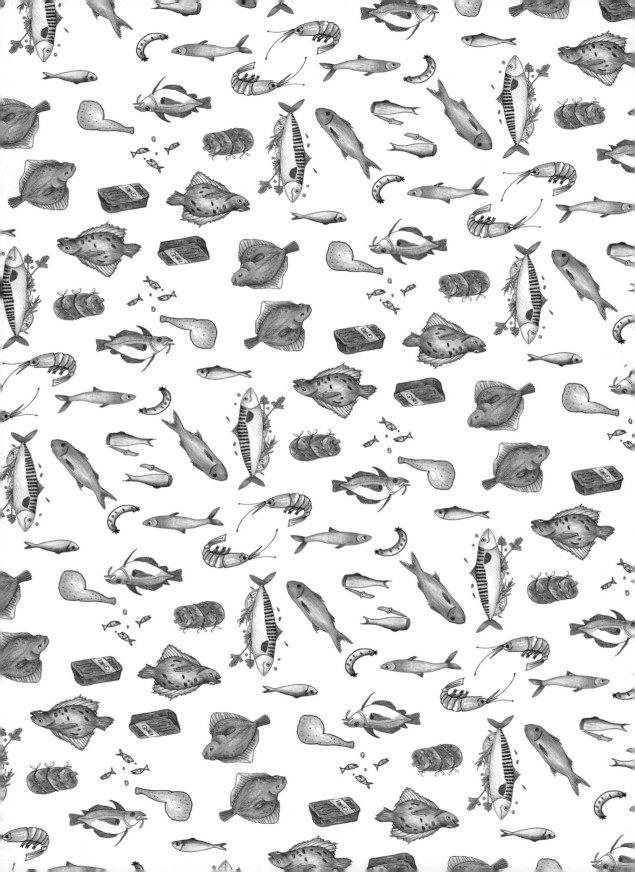

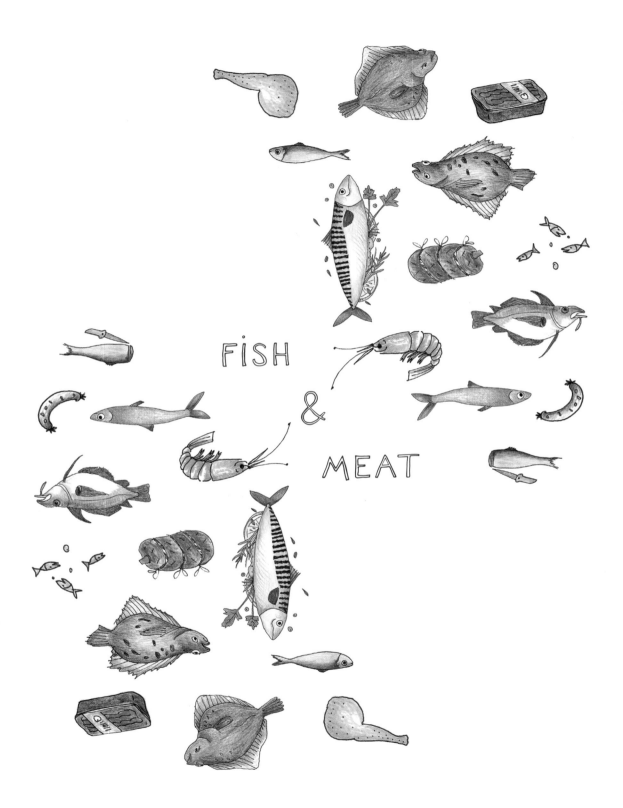

FISH

&

MEAT

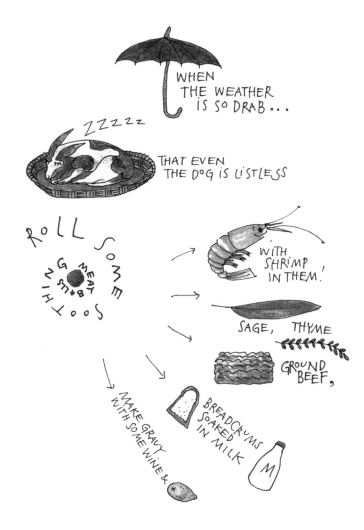

WHEN THE WEATHER IS SO DRAB...

ZZZZZ

THAT EVEN THE DOG IS LISTLESS

ROLL SOME SOOTHING MEATBALLS

WITH SHRIMP IN THEM!

SAGE, THYME

GROUND BEEF,

BREADCRUMS SOAKED IN MILK

MAKE GRAVY WITH SOME WINE &

It was a drizzly, gloomy day. Even the dog didn't want to go outside. I threw a log on the fire and thought of meatballs. They are among the most comforting edible things that exist. My father's were unparalleled; so were my mother's, but in an entirely different way. Someone from the Jordaan neighborhood in Amsterdam would create yet another kind of meatball with shrimp, to generate the umami effect, long before anyone had even heard of such a word. I combined aspects of all three, and the result was not bad at all. We ate them with a sweet potato gratin and spinach. You can find the recipe on page 15.

COMFORTING MEATBALLS

Soak the breadcrumbs in the milk for 20 minutes. Squeeze the bread and throw out the remaining milk.

Sauté the onion in a bit of oil until soft and translucent. Set aside to cool off.

In a large bowl, thoroughly knead together the breadcrumbs, onion, and all the remaining ingredients for the meatballs, seasoning with salt and pepper. Shape into 10 balls.

Fry them in oil, in a single layer, in batches if necessary, over medium heat until they are brown. Keep the balls that are ready in a baking dish under aluminum foil.

Preheat the oven to 400°F (200°C).

Make the sauce: Douse the empty meatball-cooking pan with the wine, cook to reduce slightly, then add the stock, lemon zest and juice, and thyme. Reduce slightly and pour the sauce over the meatballs in the baking dish.

Place the dish in the oven and bake the meatballs for 20 minutes, then serve.

makes 10 meatballs

¾ cup (75 g) breadcrumbs

7 tablespoons (100 ml) milk

1 onion, minced

Splash of olive oil, plus more for frying

1 pound 2 ounces (500 g) ground beef

1 egg

8 sage leaves, finely chopped

½ tablespoon fresh thyme leaves

Pinch of ground cayenne

3½ ounces (100 g) peeled small shrimp

Sea salt and freshly ground black pepper

FOR THE SAUCE

7 tablespoons (100 ml) dry white wine

1¼ cups (300 ml) chicken stock

Juice and grated zest of 1 lemon

1 tablespoon finely chopped fresh thyme or sage

MAKE A NICE SAUCE

→ HEAVY PAN

SAUTÉ ONION & GARLIC IN OLIVE OIL.

→ ADD CRUMBLED SAUSAGE MEAT,

1 + 2 CANS OF TOMATOES,

GLASS OF RED WINE →

CHILE FLAKES TO TASTE & ROSE-MARY.

MAKE LAYERS

AMPLE GRATED PARMESAN

— GRATED MOZZARELLA —

SHEET OF LASAGNA

EGG SLICES

FINELY CHOPPED SPINACH

MOZZARELLA

SHEET OF LASAGNA

TOMATO SAUCE

SHEET OF LASAGNA

ET CETERA...

One day my friend Maria, who is from Calabria, brought me a jar of pureed bell peppers and hot peppers from her sister in Italy. It had been preserved for the winter months and was meant for making Calabrian sausage. And so, we stood there on a Friday afternoon, grinding sausage meat, mixing it and casing it. Maria told me how the process went at home: The butcher came to slaughter the pig on their farm, the men chopped up the meat. With two large knives, mind you, not with a meat grinder. It tasted better that way. The women would pack the meat in the casings and tie up the sausages, all while shooting the breeze. If the stone oven was still hot from baking bread, they would make lasagna with the leftover meat. Calabrian lasagna, of course, with eggs and ham. And without the béchamel. That's what I did that night, but I replaced the ham with spinach—with Maria's approval.

MY CALABRIAN LASAGNA

In a large, heavy pan, sauté the onion and garlic in the oil for about 8 minutes over low heat. Turn up the heat, add the meat, and fry until fully cooked. Douse with the wine. Add the tomatoes, rosemary, and chile flakes and let the sauce simmer for 20 minutes over low heat. Taste and season if necessary with salt and pepper.

Preheat the oven to 350°F (180°C).

Grease a lasagna baking dish. Create layers: Start with some of the meat sauce, cover with lasagna sheets, then the spinach, egg slices, some mozzarella, more lasagna sheets, meat sauce, and so on.

Finish off with the mozzarella and sprinkle the dish with Parmesan.

Bake the lasagna for 45 minutes, or until the lasagna sheets are nicely al dente and the sauce bubbles fiercely.

serves 4

- 1 onion, finely chopped
- 3 cloves garlic, minced
- 1 tablespoon olive oil
- 1 pound 2 ounces (500 g) well-seasoned Italian pork sausages, casings removed, meat minced
- ¾ cup plus 1 tablespoon (200 ml) red wine
- 2 (14.5-ounce/411 g) cans diced tomatoes
- 1 tablespoon finely chopped fresh rosemary leaves
- Chile flakes to taste
- Sea salt and freshly ground black pepper
- 9 to 12 sheets oven-ready lasagna
- 1 pound 2 ounces (500 g) spinach, fried in a wok and chopped
- 4 hard-boiled eggs, sliced
- 8¾ ounces (250 g) mozzarella cheese, coarsely shredded
- ½ cup (50 g) finely grated Parmesan cheese

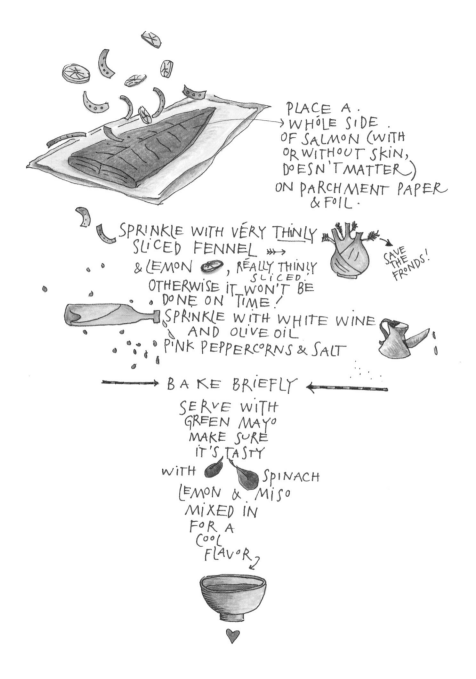

PLACE A.
WHOLE SIDE.
OF SALMON (WITH
OR WITHOUT SKIN,
DOESN'T MATTER)
ON PARCHMENT PAPER
& FOIL.

SPRINKLE WITH VERY THINLY
SLICED FENNEL ➤➤
& LEMON, REALLY THINLY
                    SLICED!
OTHERWISE IT WON'T BE
DONE ON TIME!

SAVE THE FRONDS!

SPRINKLE WITH WHITE WINE
AND OLIVE OIL
PINK PEPPERCORNS & SALT

BAKE BRIEFLY ←

SERVE WITH
GREEN MAYO
MAKE SURE
IT'S TASTY

WITH   SPINACH
LEMON & MISO
MIXED IN
FOR A
COOL
FLAVOR?

94

Assuming you too occasionally have dinner guests on the weekend, I want to introduce you to this dish. It's incredibly easy, but still kind of impressive and delicious with steamed potatoes and a salad. It's important that you bake the salmon very briefly—the top may be almost raw still, but just about warm; overcooked salmon is dry, and dull, and therefore a waste. You'll recognize the "too-far-gone" moment immediately; you'll start seeing white clotted protein on the fish. It's inevitable if you bake an entire side, which has unequal thickness, but if you cover the flat tail with fennel slices and just make sure to bake it briefly, you'll be all right.

serves 6

2 to 3 tablespoons olive oil

1 side of wild Alaskan salmon (2 pounds 3 ounces/1 kg)

Sea salt

1 lemon, very thinly sliced

1 fennel bulb, very thinly sliced (keep the fronds)

Splash of white wine

2 teaspoons crushed red peppercorns or freshly ground four seasons pepper

FOR THE MAYONNAISE

Handful of spinach

1 to 2 tablespoons fresh lemon juice

2 teaspoons white miso, or sharp prepared mustard

1 cup plus 1 tablespoon (250 ml) mayonnaise

SALMON, FENNEL & LEMON WITH SPINACH MISO-MAYO

Preheat the oven to 350°F (180°C).

Line a baking sheet with two overlapping sheets of aluminum foil. Leave a good-sized overhang. Place a sheet of parchment paper on top. Brush with oil.

Place the salmon on the parchment. Sprinkle with salt and arrange the lemon and fennel slices on top. Drizzle with the wine and sprinkle with the red peppercorns. Place another parchment sheet on top and cover with aluminum foil. Carefully tuck in the edges and fold upward to prevent any liquid from seeping out.

Place the baking sheet in the oven. Bake for 18 to 20 minutes, until the core temperature is 120°F (50°C) max.

Meanwhile, make the mayonnaise: In a blender, pulse the spinach with the lemon juice and miso until completely smooth. Stir in the mayonnaise.

Serve the salmon side whole at the table, sprinkled with chopped fennel fronds, with the green mayo on the side.

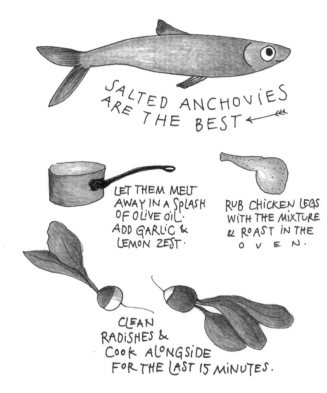

SALTED ANCHOVIES ARE THE BEST ←

LET THEM MELT AWAY IN A SPLASH OF OLIVE OIL. ADD GARLIC & LEMON ZEST.

RUB CHICKEN LEGS WITH THE MIXTURE & ROAST IN THE OVEN.

CLEAN RADISHES & COOK ALONGSIDE FOR THE LAST 15 MINUTES.

It's too cold right now, but starting in April anchovies might begin to show up in the Netherlands. Whoever thinks that anchovies only live in warmer parts of Europe is wrong. There used to be large schools of anchovies in the former Zuiderzee (a Dutch inland sea) and in the Wadden Sea. They've largely disappeared in those areas, mostly due to the Afsluitdijk, a dike that turned the Zuiderzee into a lake. But they still live in the Oosterschelde, a large saltwater body that used to be an estuary. They come to spawn on the higher-lying sand-banks—where the water is just a bit warmer—and prefer to do it in brackish water, like in the Oosterschelde. In Bergen op Zoom they still catch anchovies the traditional way, and as soon as the fish has arrived, people are spoiling for a bag of fresh ones, or for salted anchovies from the Van Dort fishing family. A true delicacy.

serves 4

1 (2-ounce/55 g) can anchovy fillets

3 tablespoons olive oil

3 to 4 cloves garlic, minced

Juice and grated zest of 1 lemon

Freshly ground black pepper

4 chicken leg quarters

2 to 3 bunches radishes, trimmed and washed, big ones halved

1 tablespoon butter

Generous ¼ cup (15 g) chopped fresh flat-leaf parsley

A baguette, sliced, for serving (optional)

CHiCKEN WiTH ANCHOViES & LiTTLE RADiSHES

Cook the anchovies in the oil over low heat until they dissolve, about 5 minutes. Remove from the heat and stir in the garlic and lemon zest. Grind in some pepper.

Rub the chicken legs with the mixture and place them, with dripping oil and all, in a baking dish. Ideally let marinate for about 30 minutes, or continue straightaway.

Preheat the oven to 350°F (180°C).

Bake the legs for 40 to 45 minutes. Then add the radishes to the dish and spoon them into the fat.

Bake for another 10 to 15 minutes, until they are just about ready. Douse the dish with some lemon juice, add a dab of butter to the pan, stir, and sprinkle generously with parsley.

Delicious served with baguette to soak up the anchovy oil.

→ MASHED POTATOES LEFTOVERS

+

MIXED MINCED MEATS , ONIONS , BOUILLON CUBE ,

CLOVES , CORI AN DER , KECAP , SAMBAL ,

GIN- GER , LIME , EGGS ,

MILK & HANDFUL OF BREADCRUMBS

all together makes frikadel pan!

There are as many recipes for *frikadel pan* as for Bolognese sauce. It's an Indo-European comfort food that's a curious melting pot of Indonesian and Dutch cuisine. Most likely, its appearance in Indonesia was a result of Dutch food culture's influence. The word *frikadel* is old Dutch or Flemish for meatball, and it resurfaces in Indonesian cuisine as a name for the same dish, either with or without the addition of vegetables like potatoes or corn. *Frikadel* can be a small ball or an entire loaf. How the Spanish word *pan* (bread) came to be part of it is a mystery to me, though. Maybe it's actually a meatloaf that's being baked in an oven dish (a pan!). Speak up if you know the answer. Whatever it may be, it's a fantastic and ridiculously easy, finger-licking-good dish.

serves 6

2 pounds 3 ounces (1 kg) ground meat (half beef, half pork)

2 small onions, diced

1 beef bouillon cube, crumbled

2 cloves, crushed

2 teaspoons coriander seeds, crushed

3 tablespoons kecap manis, plus extra for the sauce

2 tablespoons sambal terasi, plus extra for the sauce

1 inch (2.5 cm) fresh ginger, finely grated

Juice and grated zest of 1 lime

2 eggs, beaten

½ cup plus 1 teaspoon (125 ml) milk

1¼ cups (300 g) coarsely mashed cooked potatoes

Handful (approx. ¾ cup) of breadcrumbs (if needed)

1 tablespoon sunflower or canola oil, for greasing the baking sheet

FRiKADEL PAN (iNDO-DUTCH MEATLOAF)

Preheat the oven to 350°F (180°C).

In a large bowl, combine the ground meat with the onions, the crushed bouillon cube, the crushed spices, kecap, sambal, ginger, and lime zest.

Beat the eggs with the milk and stir into the mixture. Fold in the potatoes. No need to smooth everything, it's fine to see some potato. If it's too wet, add some breadcrumbs.

Shape into a round loaf and place on a rimmed baking sheet greased with oil, and bake the frikadel pan for about 1 hour, until cooked through. The internal temperature should be at least 155°F (68°C); it will continue to rise to 160°F (71°C) as it stands. Let stand for 10 minutes.

Whisk together kecap, sambal, and lime juice to taste to make a sauce, brush it onto the meatloaf, and serve.

Note: Sambal terasi is an Indonesian hot sauce (sambal) with a fermented fish (terasi) flavor. Kecap manis is an Indonesian sweet soy sauce. Both are available at Asian markets or online.

PASILLA IS A MILD
AROMATIC PEPPER
THAT YOU NEED TO
SOAK. OTHERWISE PICK
A REGULAR ONE!

CHIPOTLE PEPPERS
ARE SMOKED &
DRIED JALAPEÑOS
AND THEREFORE
NOT VERY SPICY.
SUBSTITUTE REGULAR
JALAPEÑOS & SMOKED
PAPRIKA.

SIMPLY BUY
THEM CANNED,
THOUGH!

(REFRIGERATED, THEY
KEEP FOREVER)

Chocolate originally comes from Mesoamerica, where the Aztecs and Maya were known to use cacao beans as a means of payment or for making a drink since forever. No wonder that they cooked with it. Cacao by itself isn't sweet. It has a deep, rich flavor that works well with roasted meat.

Many chefs in proper, old-fashioned Dutch restaurants in the country use cacao—or chocolate sauce—combined with wild game, like deer meat. But real savory cacao with roasted meat truly is an eye-opener. For this recipe, I use cacao nibs, which are available in most grocery stores on the "superfood" shelves. Cacao nibs are basically crushed, toasted cacao beans. These completely lack the sweetness of a chocolate bar, but in combination with the rich flavor of smoked peppers and roasted (or stewed) meat, they are a savory staple in my Meso-american repertoire.

serves 4

3 tablespoons olive oil

1 pasilla pepper (or red chile pepper), rehydrated if dried

4 chipotles in adobe sauce; or 4 jalapeños plus 1 teaspoon smoked paprika

3 tablespoons honey

4 clove garlic, chopped

3 tablespoons cacao nibs, plus 1 to 2 tablespoons extra for sprinkling

Juice of 1 lime

Sea salt

1 pound 10 ounces (750 g) pork belly, in one piece

ROASTED CHOCOLATE PORK BELLY

Preheat the oven to 300°F (150°C).

Heat the oil in a saucepan and sauté the peppers, honey, and garlic. Let simmer for 10 minutes over low heat.

Add the cacao nibs and season with lime juice and salt. In a food processor, blender, or with a hand blender, process into a more or less thin, smooth paste. Rub the pork belly with the paste. Place in a baking dish and cover with aluminum foil.

Place in the oven and bake for 2 hours. Remove the foil and bake for another 20 to 30 minutes, until a knife effortlessly slides through the meat and it has a nice golden brown crust.

Using a mortar and pestle or a food processor, grind another 1 to 2 tablespoons cacao nibs to a coarse powder. Cut the meat into thick slices, sprinkle with cacao, and serve.

In the Netherlands, when a fisherman is fishing for common sole, only 15 percent of the entire catch is actually sole. The rest consists of countless other flatfish and other kinds of fish. Isn't it ridiculous that we throw back delicious fish, just because it doesn't get sold?

Recently I was at the Albert Cuyp street market in Amsterdam, shopping at a stand filled to the brim with fish. I asked the fishmonger which fish was bycatch, and he lifted up a good-looking fat dab. It was dirt cheap and he even gutted and filleted it for me. Your fishmonger is happy to help, but you really need to ask him. Besides dab, choose whiting, gray gurnard, pouting, or lemon sole. They're all on the boat and taste just as delicious as (and are often lots cheaper than) every other white fish that you're more familiar with.

serves 4

- 3½ tablespoons (50 g) butter, plus some extra, at room temperature
- 3 tablespoons coarse prepared mustard
- Sea salt and freshly ground black pepper
- Generous ½ cup (75 g) hazelnuts, toasted until crunchy in a dry skillet
- 2 large or 4 small white fish fillets, ideally bycatch
- Handful of fresh garden herbs, such as thyme leaves, arugula, and so on

BYCATCH WITH NUT BUTTER

Cream the butter with the mustard. Season with salt and pepper. Chop the nuts (this can be done very quickly in a food processor), and fold them in. Spread a thick layer of nut butter on top of the fish. Let stiffen in the fridge for 1 hour.

Preheat the oven to 400°F (200°C), then turn on the broiler.

Grease a broiler-proof baking dish with some butter and lay down the fish with the nut butter side facing up. Depending on the thickness of the fillets, bake for about 7 minutes, until just flaky. Sprinkle with the herbs and serve.

TIP TO QUICKLY SOAK
DRIED BEANS &
CHICKPEAS

PLACE THE BEANS OR
PEAS IN A SAUCEPAN.
COVER WITH WATER BY
ABOUT 2 INCHES. (5CM)

BRING TO A BOIL
IMMEDIATELY REMOVE
PAN FROM HEAT.
LET STAND FOR AT LEAST
1 HOUR (BUT NOT OVERNIGHT)

DRAIN AND
COOK THE BEANS
IN FRESH WATER
UNTIL TENDER.

→ VOILA ←

I brought a container of black chickpeas back from Italy. I'd never seen them in real life, so that's why I immediately bought them. Black chickpeas are ancient and only grow in the south of Italy and India. The ones from India are smaller, but they are no doubt related. They are beautiful black beads that demand some patience; you'll easily need an additional day to presoak them. If you're not in a hurry, I strongly recommend that you soak and precook the chickpeas yourself. Canned chickpeas can't live up to the sensation offered by the bite of dried and home-cooked chickpeas. In the poorer southern regions of Italy, black chickpeas were commonly used as a meat replacement since they are rich in protein and iron (as are yellow chickpeas). You can find black chickpeas online very easily, otherwise just use yellow ones. If you'd like, you can make the following recipe without fish and instead double the quantity of chickpeas. It's up to you.

SPINACH, COCONUT & CHICKPEA FISH STEW

Preheat the oven to 400°F (200°C).

Heat the ghee in a heavy ovenproof saucepan over medium heat. Add the onion and sauté for about 5 minutes, then add the garlic, ginger, lemon zest, and chile flakes. Fry for about 3 minutes, stirring.

Add the chickpeas and the fish, place the spinach on top, and pour the coconut milk over it. Season with salt and pepper. Place the pan without the lid in the oven for 20 minutes. Slide in the pita breads directly on the rack for the final 5 minutes. Remove from the oven and stir the cilantro into the stew.

Slice the pita breads open, scoop in the stew, and serve immediately.

serves 4 to 5

2 teaspoons ghee or olive oil

1 onion, diced

4 cloves garlic, minced

1 tablespoon grated fresh ginger

Juice and grated zest of 1 lemon

Pinch of chile flakes

14-ounces (400 g) precooked dried chickpeas

1 pound 2 ounces (500 g) white fish (ideally Marine Stewardship Council/MSC label), cubed

7 ounces (200 g) spinach, preferably wild

1 (3.5-ounce/400 ml) can coconut milk

Sea salt and freshly ground black pepper

4 or 5 large pita breads

1 bunch fresh cilantro (½ ounce/15 g), coarsely chopped

PERNOD REALLY ADS A FINISHING TOUCH TO YOUR MEDITERRANEAN FISH PIE.

(YOU CAN FINISH OFF THE REST OF THE BOTTLE)

↓

RICARD IS FINE AS WELL

THE ENTIRE CATCH GETS PIE-FACED!

Well, I figured I'd give you another recipe for bycatch. When fishing for one specific kind, fishermen also catch a host of other fish species in their big nets. But since we are less familiar with those serendipitous fish, they don't sell. A shame. So today we're making a lovely fish stew from southern France that requires all kinds of bycatch. When you're on vacation, don't you enjoy a nice bowl of bouillabaisse? It's basically use-your-bycatch soup! Add a nice pastry cover and it becomes a serious dish!

MEDITERRANEAN FISH POTPIE

Preheat the oven to 400°F (200°C).

Heat the oil in a large pan over medium heat. Add the onion and sauté until translucent. Add the fennel and the garlic and fry for 3 to 4 minutes. Stir in the tomato puree and the spices, and fry until it starts to emanate a sweet aroma. Douse the pan with a glass of Pernod. Reduce somewhat, and pour in the stock. Bring everything to a boil and let simmer over low heat for about 12 minutes, until the fennel is al dente. Season with salt and pepper to taste.

Remove from the heat. Nestle the fish and peas into the sauce and place everything in a baking dish. Roll out the puff pastry to the size of the dish, prick a hole in the middle, brush some egg wash over the rim of the dish, and place the dough on top of the baking dish. Decorate and brush the dough with the remainder of the egg. Bake the fish stew in the oven for 25 to 30 minutes, until the pastry is golden. Serve.

serves 4

2 tablespoons olive oil

1 onion, diced

1 fennel bulb, with fronds, chopped

2 cloves garlic, minced

2½ ounces tomato paste

Pinch of saffron

½ tablespoon fennel seeds, crushed in a mortar

½ tablespoon coriander seeds, crushed in a mortar

About ½ cup (125 ml) Pernod or Ricard

Scant 1½ cups (350 ml) fish stock

Sea salt and freshly ground black pepper

1 pound 9 ounces (700 g) haddock or a mix of bycatch (dab, gurnard, and so on)

1⅓ cups (200 g) green peas

8¾ ounces (250 g) puff pastry

1 egg, beaten

STUFF FRESH
MACKERELS
WITH
LEMON
AND A PASTE
MADE FROM
DILL, PARSLEY
CUMIN, CORIANDER
SEEDS, GARLIC, OLIVE
OIL, CHILES, SALT & PEPPER.
COVER
AND BAKE
UNTIL DONE.

Mackerel is a real summer fish. They spawn in spring, west of Ireland, and then they swim in giant schools to the North Sea. They are real hunters that swim just below sea level. I've once fished for them myself. We kept an eye on the seagulls. Wherever they circled above the water, that's where the mackerel swam. Both on the prowl.

With a little boat, we glided closer and bounced our fishing rods, the lines decorated with glimmering pieces of shiny foil, up and down in the water. I had to keep moving to fool the mackerels and make them bite. Sometimes I caught four at once!

In early June, you can find mackerel at your fishmonger. It's an inexpensive fish, but make sure to check the sustainability label. And eat the fish the same day; because it's a fatty fish, it can quickly turn rancid.

SPICED MACKEREL

Preheat the oven to 400°F (200°C).

Crush—ideally in a mortar—the garlic and salt into a paste. Add the chile flakes, coriander, and cumin and then the parsley and grind again, adding a drop of oil to make the paste slightly more runny.

Rinse the fish and dab dry with paper towel. Sprinkle the cavity of the fish with salt. Grease a baking dish and lay the fish inside.

Arrange the lemon slices in the cavities and spread the parsley paste over the lemons. Pour another drop of oil over the mackerels and wrap the dish in aluminum foil.

Bake for 20 minutes, depending on the size of the fish. Sprinkle with lemon juice, garnish with lemon slices and parsley, if desired, and serve.

serves 4

3 large cloves garlic

1 teaspoon sea salt, plus extra

Pinch of chile flakes, to taste

1 teaspoon coriander seeds

½ teaspoon cumin seeds

¼ cup (10 g) finely chopped fresh flat-leaf parsley, plus extra for garnish

Nice olive oil

4 mackerels, cleaned (ask your fishmonger)

2 lemons, 1 thinly sliced and the juice of the other, plus extra for garnish

CLOUD EGGS

SEPARATE THE EGGS AND KEEP THE YOLKS IN INDIVIDUAL CUPS OR GLASSES.

BEAT THE EGG WHITES UNTIL STIFF.

FOLD IN SOME GREEN HERBS, OR CHEESE OR HAM...

ON A BAKING SHEET, FORM CLOUDS WITH A WELL (FOR THE YOLK) BAKE 6 TO 8 MINUTES.

ADD THE YOLKS & BAKE VERY BRIEFLY.

BREATHTAKING BREAKFAST

Well, Van Boven joined the breakfast trend. Some dishes suddenly go viral and then all of social media features the same recipe. I was eating avocados long before Instagram was founded. And I don't even want to try those repulsive things like sushi donuts, waffle pops, and anything that includes the word *unicorn*, in rainbow colors and chock-full of sugar: unicorn farts (meringues), frappuccinos, sundaes. And then cloud eggs popped up. That sounded really wonderful, and guess what: They are delicious! Hearty meringues for Sunday morning that radiate like the sun—I get why the entire world is won over. They are super easy; you don't need more than an egg, but if you have a slice of ham leftover, or enough herbs from your garden for breakfast, you can use those too. Let's all enjoy the hippest breakfast in the social media universe!

CLOUD EGG

serves 1

1 egg, separated

Sea salt

Drop of fresh lemon juice or vinegar

½ tablespoon finely chopped fresh garden herbs

1 tablespoon finely grated Parmesan cheese, ham slivers, or finely chopped smoked salmon

Freshly ground black pepper

Preheat the oven to 435°F (225°C). Line a baking sheet with a sheet of parchment paper.

If you make several at once; keep each yolk aside in its own cup.

Whip the egg white with a pinch of salt and 1 drop lemon juice until stiff, like a meringue. Once it's stiff, fold in the herbs and the cheese, ham, or salmon. Not too much, or it will deflate. Just a bit for flavor.

Scoop a cloud of the egg white onto the prepared baking sheet and with the back of a spoon, make an indentation in the middle where you'll place your yolk later. When using multiple eggs, make multiple clouds.

Place the cloud in the oven for 6 to 8 minutes; you can decide for yourself whether you'd like it more crunchy or paler. Slide the yolk into the well and bake for another 2 to 3 minutes. Grind pepper on top. Serve.

SLICE OFF TOP & BOTTOM

SEASON THE PORK WITH THE RUB & CHOPPED PINEAPPLE

STUFF THE PINEAPPLE WITH IT!

HALVE, PEEL & REMOVE

THAT HARD CORE

HOLLOW OUT A LITTLE MORE SPRINKLE WITH —— RUB ——

WRAP THE WHOLE THING IN BACON (I WEAVE THE STRIPS) AND GRILL SLOW & LOW SERVE WITH CAP AND BOTTOM!

I was browsing my mother's recipe archive for inspiration. What did we eat in the 1970s when I was growing up in Ireland? I found handwritten recipes for "chicken mulligatawny" (some sort of curry chicken with lemon slices), banana with ham and cheese sauce, grapefruit cocktail, fried pineapple slices with rum and ham, onions filled with ground beef and stem ginger, curry of liver with caraway and raisins. Anyway, you get the point. Fruit was hot. I looked closer at the pineapple recipe. It didn't sound that terrible. It made me think of the American recipe for swineapple—a slow-roasted pineapple filled with spicy pork shoulder (nowadays we call it pulled pork) coated with crispy bacon—and I immediately made it for dinner that night. Believe me, it was finger-licking good. The '70s weren't so bad.

makes 1 stuffed pineapple; serves 3 or 4

FOR THE RUB

2 tablespoons packed dark brown sugar

1 to 2 tablespoons chili powder

2 tablespoons prepared mustard

2 tablespoons curry powder

2 tablespoons coriander seeds, crushed with a mortar and pestle

1 tablespoon dried oregano

3 to 4 tablespoons paprika

1 tablespoon salt

1 large pineapple

1 pound 2 ounces (500 g) pork shoulder, cubed

8¾ ounces (250 g) thickly sliced bacon (about 12 slices)

SWINEAPPLE

Preheat the oven to 300°F (150°C). Line a baking sheet with parchment paper.

Make the rub: Combine all the ingredients in a bowl and set aside.

Remove the top and bottom from the pineapple, but don't throw them out. Peel the outside, halve the pineapple lengthwise, and remove the hard core. Hollow out a little more and keep the flesh.

Sprinkle the entire pineapple with some of the rub. Combine the meat with the remaining finely chopped pineapple and season with the rest of the rub. Scoop into one half of the pineapple, and press the other half on top.

Wrap the whole pineapple in slices of bacon (I braided them) and secure them with bamboo skewers. Place the entire contraption on the baking sheet and cover with aluminum foil.

Roast the pineapple for 3 hours. Remove the foil and roast for another 30 minutes. Decorate with the reserved top and bottom of the pineapple. Eat with baguette and herb butter.

EAT YOUR GYROS ON WHICHEVER BREAD YOU LIKE

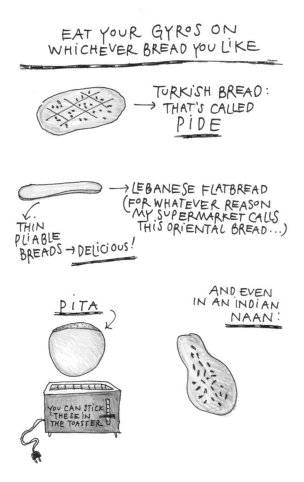

→ TURKISH BREAD: THAT'S CALLED PIDE

→ LEBANESE FLATBREAD (FOR WHATEVER REASON MY SUPERMARKET CALLS THIS ORIENTAL BREAD...)

THIN PLIABLE BREADS → DELICIOUS!

PITA

AND EVEN IN AN INDIAN NAAN:

YOU CAN STICK THESE IN THE TOASTER

The Greek street food gyro is made with strips of well-seasoned lamb, chicken, or pork meat that's rolled into flatbread with some sauce, tomato, lettuce, and onion. You could say it most resembles a shawarma sandwich from the Middle East or a taco al pastor from Mexico because they all depend on the seasoning and cooking method: The seasoned meat is stacked in thin layers on a vertical spit, sometimes interspersed with fat trimmings, and roasted in front of a fire. All of these variations cooked on the vertical rotisserie appear to come from the Turkish döner kebab (*döner* = rotating; *kebab* = marinated meat). The döner sandwich—originally without all the extras, like sauce, tomato, and so on—is actually not so old. The Turkish immigrant worker Kadir Norman introduced his döner, strips of lamb scooped into Turkish bread, in Berlin only in 1972.

CHiCKEN GYRo WRAPS

Make the mint tzatziki: Grate the cucumber. Combine with some salt and let drain for 15 minutes in a colander. Squeeze out the liquid. Combine the grated cucumber with the rest of the ingredients and let stand for 1 hour in the fridge.

Preheat the oven to 400°F (200°C).

Place the chicken thighs on a cutting board, smooth side down, and cut a few deep slashes in each. Place them between two sheets of plastic wrap and flatten them using some heavy object. Grind the oregano and spices with some salt and pepper in a mortar and rub the mixture into the meat.

Heat a splash of oil in a rimmed baking sheet in the oven.

Place the flattened chicken thighs on the hot baking sheet and bake for 15 minutes, until they are tender, flipping them halfway through the cooking time. Slide in the pita breads a few minutes before the chicken is done. Halve the breads, fill them with tomato and lettuce if you wish, a chicken thigh, and lots of tzatziki, and serve.

serves 4

FOR THE MINT TZATZIKI

1 cucumber

Sea salt

1 clove garlic, pressed

1 bunch fresh mint (½ ounce/15 g), chopped very finely

1¼ cups (300 ml) plain Greek yogurt

FOR THE WRAPS

1 pound 5 ounces (600 g) boneless, skinless chicken thighs

2 teaspoons dried oregano or thyme

1 teaspoon each fennel seeds, cumin seeds, smoked paprika

Pinch of chili powder

Sea salt and freshly ground black pepper

1½ tablespoons olive oil

4 large pita breads

Tomato and lettuce, if desired

HEAT

SOME OLIVE OIL IN A
DUTCH OVEN
GIVE THE TENTACLES
A SCARE!

BOO!

ADD GARLIC
← WINE,
A CHILE

VIN

WATER OR
BROTH

PLACE IN A PREHEATED
OVEN: BRAISE UNTIL TENDER

I've been increasingly seeing fresh octopus at the fishmonger or in good-quality grocery stores. This is fun, as it means you can dare to prepare it and eat it more frequently. Admittedly, they look a little slippery, those tentacles, but don't let yourself be deterred. You only have to braise them. Depending on the quantity and thickness of the tentacles, you should braise them for 1 to 3 hours. It helps to have a bit of acidity in your liquid, so braising in wine works great. Stories about adding a copper coin or cork to your liquid have made the rounds, but food writer Harold McGee, whom I trust without a shadow of doubt, has not been able to find scientific proof for this. So don't let yourself be fooled, just braise them in wine and throw in some other delicious ingredient. Eat the tentacles while still warm, sliced and seasoned with a peppery olive oil, sprinkled with smoked paprika, and served with a steamed potato. Or, like I just did, sliced and combined with fregola (toasted pasta balls), fresh green peas, finely grated fennel, and radicchio.

serves 4

2 tablespoons olive oil

2 to 3 octopus tentacles, head removed

4 cloves garlic, sliced

1 (750 ml) bottle white or red wine

Sea salt

1 small red chile pepper

TACKLING TENTACLES

Preheat the oven to 400°F (200°C).

Heat the oil in a heavy ovenproof cast-iron pan with a lid. Fry the tentacles all over for 2 to 3 minutes. Add the garlic, stir for a minute, then douse the tentacles with the wine. Add enough water to properly submerge the tentacles. Season with salt and add the red pepper. Once the liquid boils, put the lid on the pan and braise the octopus in the oven for 1 to 1½ hours.

Test the flesh for doneness. It should be tender, as cooking it for too long makes it tough. Rinse off the tentacles and serve as you prefer.

GRATE ZUCCHINI

COLLECT IN
A CLEAN CLOTH
(PLACED INSIDE
A COLANDER)
SPRINKLE WITH SALT,
AND LET STAND.

SQUEEZE!

AND FRY
WITH AN ONION...

BEAT EGGS
ALONG WITH
SOME MILK...

AND ADD TO THE PAN

TURN OFF
THE HEAT,
AND TURN ON
THE OVEN.
SPOON RICOTTA
ONTO THE FRITTATA
& CRUMBLE THE 'NDUJA
ON TOP → BAKE!

BEFORE SERVING, GARNISH
WITH LOTS & LOTS OF
FRESH HERBS.

My friend Maria returned from a visit to her homeland Calabria, located in the toe of Italy's boot, and brought back a large chunk of 'nduja—a Calabrian sausage—for me. Out of all the sausages in the world, 'nduja is my all-time favorite. It's a spreadable salami that is made of the fatty parts of the pork and seasoned with herbs and spices, specifically with paprika and lots of chile peppers. Outside of Italy, it's available in some Italian specialty stores, or online. Otherwise you may substitute very finely chopped chorizo, even though it's by far not as spicy and well seasoned as the real deal. It works wonderfully as a pizza topping (yes!), or fried in a pan with cockles or mussels, and is delicious on this zucchini frittata. Frittata with 'nduja . . . hallelujah.

ZUCCHINI FRITTATA WITH 'NDUJA

Preheat the oven to 350°F (180°C).

Spread out the grated zucchini on a clean dish towel in a colander and sprinkle with a pinch of salt. Let stand for 10 minutes. Squeeze out the zucchini.

In an ovenproof pan, sauté the onion in the oil, add the zucchini, and fry, stirring, for about 8 minutes.

Beat the eggs with some milk, salt, and pepper. Pour into the pan. Stir to equally distribute the zucchini and onion. Remove from the heat.

Dollop the ricotta on top. Crumble the 'nduja over it and slide the pan into the oven. Bake for about 15 minutes, until just set. Let cool for 5 minutes. Grate lemon zest over the frittata and sprinkle with herbs. Cut into wedges. Serve.

serves 4 for lunch (with bread), or 2 as a dinner main course

2 big zucchini, coarsely grated

Sea salt

1 onion, diced

2 tablespoons olive oil

6 large eggs

Splash of milk

Freshly ground black pepper

5 tablespoons (75 ml) ricotta

2 tablespoons 'nduja or chorizo, crumbled

Grated zest of 1 lemon

Handful of fresh herbs, like basil, chives, parsley, and nasturtium flowers

DISOBEDIENT PIE

BOIL WATER & BUTTER. ADD THE FLOUR IN 1 SWOOP.

SHAPE INTO A SOFT BALL.

SAUTÉ A BATCH OF RED ONIONS UNTIL BUTTERY SMOOTH.

FILL A PREBAKED PIE CRUST WITH THE ONIONS

TOP WITH SARDINES

HOME MADE PICKLED FISH IS THE BEST!

MIX IN SOME ONIONS!

FINISH THE PIE! CHECK!

The crust for this tart is briefly cooked before topping. This makes it fantastically pliable, so it keeps its shape when you spread on the hot filling. It's actually my recipe for English pie dough, and an English savory filling such as pork pie also works really well. But I still had some pickled sardines in my fridge, and wanted to make something nice with them: a variation on the French pissaladière. If you don't have pickled sardines, you can use salted anchovies instead. In fact, that's the traditional recipe! But who ever does what they're supposed to do anymore?

PISSALADIÈRE

Preheat the oven to 350°F (180°C).

Heat ¾ cup (175 ml) water with the butter in a saucepan until the butter has melted. Throw in all of the flour at once, add a pinch of salt, and combine into a firm large ball. On the counter, knead it into a smooth, consistent dough. Flatten somewhat and allow to cool off. On the counter, roll out the dough into a flat slab that would fit a shallow, greased 9½-inch (24 cm) cake pan. Fit the dough in the pan, trim the edges, and poke a couple of holes in the bottom with a fork.

Prebake the crust in the oven for 15 minutes.

Meanwhile, sauté the onions in the olive oil until soft and sweet: Fry them over medium heat and take your time. Stir occasionally. Season with the oregano, pepper, and a bit of salt.

Spread the onions over the crust. Arrange the fish fillets on top herringbone style and place the olives on top.

Bake the pissaladière for about 25 minutes, until nicely browned, then slice and serve.

makes 1 tart

3½ tablespoons (50 g) butter, plus extra for greasing the pan

1¾ cups (225 g) spelt flour

Pinch of sea salt

1¾ pounds (800 g) red onion, thinly sliced

5 tablespoons (75 ml) olive oil

1½ teaspoons dried oregano

Freshly ground black pepper

1 to 2 cans salted anchovy fillets or sardines, drained

A couple of nice olives, pitted

MAKING MEATLOAF
IS SO EASY:
(THIS IS A BASIC RECIPE
ADJUST TO YOUR
OWN TASTE)

2 POUNDS (1KG)
GROUND BEEF

MUSTARD

ORANGE
ZEST

HOISIN
(OR KECAP)

THYME

→ 1 EGG

KNEAD INTO
A NICE DOUGH →

PLACE 3
HARD-BOILED
EGGS ON
TOP.

PRESS ONE
HALF INTO A
BREAD PAN.

PRESS THE REST
ON TOP & BAKE!

So we've recently moved and now live among Manhattan-like canyons of boxes, which serve surprisingly well as a coffee table, cabinet, or trashcan. I spent a weekend organizing the storage closet and it's finally well arranged. Bottles, cleaning supplies, and pantry items are neatly stacked—oh, so convenient, just like an IKEA catalog. While shifting jars back and forth I discovered that I own an astronomical supply of piccalilli and other relishes. My new resolution: using them, instead of saving them for later. And how best to use a jar of hearty relish? Well, with the meatloaf on this page. A big one, so that you might, just like I did, go through two jars.

makes 1 large loaf; serves about 6

1 pound (500 g) ground beef

1 pound (500 g) ground pork

9½ tablespoons (150 g) Dijon-style mustard

3 to 4 tablespoons hoisin sauce or kecap manis (sweet Indonesian soy sauce)

Leaves from 4 fresh thyme sprigs

Grated zest of 1 orange

1 egg

Handful of breadcrumbs

Sea salt and freshly ground black pepper

3 hard-boiled eggs

Chutney or relish, for serving

MEATLOAF

Preheat the oven to 350°F (180°C). Grease a 9" × 5" (23 cm × 13 cm) loaf pan and line it with a large sheet of parchment paper, letting the edges overhang.

Knead all ingredients except the hard-boiled egg into a nice mixture that is no longer sticky. If it's still sticky, add some more breadcrumbs. Season generously with salt and pepper; the flavor will mellow out after baking.

Press half of the dough into the prepared pan. Peel the eggs and place them on top. Cover with the rest of the dough. Tap the pan on the counter a few times to let the air bubbles out.

Place the pan on a baking sheet (to catch any drippings) and bake the meatloaf for about 1 hour. Drain the liquid from the top, let rest for a moment, and lift out of the pan with the parchment paper.

Serve with chutney or relish.

TIE A GOOD
QUALITY
LAMB RACK.
CARVE SLITS
INTO THE MEAT
TO FIT
GARLIC SLICES

SEASON THE LAMB
SURROUND IT
WITH ONION HALVES

↓

POUR IN
HOME MADE
BROTH.
ROAST.

WHIP UP A SAUCE.
FROM PARSLEY,
MINT, ALMONDS,
LEMON & A
SPLASH OF OLIVE
OIL - P & S.

We've tentatively begun to do some holiday cooking, which is why I start with a leg of lamb in November. It's important to buy good-quality lamb. It seems logical, but not all lambs were created equal, and cheap lamb is often (almost) fully grown sheep. A big difference. Your lamb's origin also affects its flavor. Furthermore, a meat thermometer is essential when making this dish; stick it into the thickest part of the leg. Depending on several factors your lamb can take less or more time to cook. Check the temperature after 40 minutes to 1 hour and keep checking until you are pleased with the result.

serves 6

FESTIVE LAMB

Preheat the oven to 350°F (180°C).

Carve slits in the lamb and stud these with garlic slices. Rub the entire leg with salt and pepper. Place in a roasting pan with the onions and the stock and put in the oven.

Bake for 40 minutes to 1 hour, depending on the thickness of the meat; occasionally baste with the stock. When the core temperature reads 150°F (65°C), the meat is nicely rosé.

Meanwhile, make the herb sauce: Grind the parsley, mint, almond flour, oil, lemon juice, and salt and pepper to taste in a food processor.

Remove the leg from the pan and keep warm under aluminum foil. Place the pan on the stovetop over high heat and douse the meat drippings with some extra stock (or wine or liquor). Stir everything loose and season the gravy with salt and pepper as it reduces.

Cut off the butcher's twine from around the leg and remove the bone. Cut the leg into thin slices and pour the gravy over it. Serve with the onions and herb sauce.

Note: After roasting, always cover the meat and let rest for about 15 minutes.

1 leg of lamb (3 to 3½ pounds/ 1½ kg), ideally cut off the bone, with the bone placed back and tied up (ask your butcher)

8 to 10 cloves garlic, sliced

Sea salt and freshly ground black pepper

6 to 8 onions, peeled and halved

1¼ cups (300 ml) homemade stock, plus extra

FOR THE HERB SAUCE

1 bunch fresh parsley

1 bunch fresh mint

Handful of almond flour

Splash of olive oil

Squeeze of fresh lemon juice

RARE: 122 TO 126°F (50 TO 52°C)

MEDIUM-RARE: 130 TO 135°F (54 TO 57°C)

MEDIUM: 135 TO 154°F (57 TO 68°C)

WELL-DONE: 158°F (70°C)

BLANCH
LEAVES FROM
A GREEN
CABBAGE → ♥

STUFF WITH
A SIZEABLE
MEATBALL.

REMOVE THE TOUGHEST
PART OF THE STEM.

SECURE
EVERYTHING
WITH STRIPS
OF BACON.

OVERLAP THE
TWO FLAPS,
FORMING A
CABBAGE
BOWL.

STEW THE
STUFFED
CABBAGE LEAVES
IN BEER
IN THE OVEN!

Recently it was time for a new roasting pan. I had cooked away the bottom of my old pan. I know they're supposed to last a lifetime, but I used my Dutch ovens so intensely that the enamel had separated from the bottom after twenty years. It was sad, as I really loved my big orange friend. We've been through a lot together, given that a Dutch oven typically serves comfort food. And now I had to exchange him for a shiny red Le Creuset pan. It felt cruel, but life is hard. My new red friend proudly stood on the counter that night. I inaugurated him with meatballs, so that he'd immediately know who he was dealing with.

SMALL CHOU FARCIS

Preheat the oven to 400°F (200°C).

In a big pot of boiling salted water, cook the cabbage leaves for about 5 minutes. Rinse with cold water and let drain on a dish towel. Remove the tough part of the stem.

Pour the milk into a shallow bowl and let the breadcrumbs soak in it. Squeeze them slightly and add to the ground pork and beef. Knead with the shallots, mustard, Worcestershire sauce, and egg into a consistent mixture; add 1½ teaspoons salt and pepper to taste. Divide into six big balls.

Fold each cabbage leaf into a "bowl" by overlapping the sliced open seams; place a meatball inside each. Put the filled cabbage leaves in a roasting pan and add two slices of bacon over each ball, in a cross shape.

Add the beer and place the pan without the lid in the oven for 35 to 40 minutes, until the meat is cooked through.

Serve with mashed potatoes and with the beer gravy from the pan.

makes 6 balls

6 nice Savoy cabbage leaves

1¼ cups (300 ml) milk

1½ cups (140 g) dried breadcrumbs

5¼ ounces (150 g) ground pork

1 pound 7 ounces (650 g) ground beef

2 French *echalions* (banana shallots), diced

3 tablespoons prepared mustard

3 tablespoons Worcestershire sauce

1 egg, beaten

Sea salt and freshly ground black pepper

6 strips bacon, cut in half crosswise

1 (12-ounce/355 ml) bottle bock beer (or other strong lager)

FISH PIE
WITH
TENDER LEEKS

COOK POTATOES
MASH THEM
WITH BUTTER, CREAM
& CHEESE

CUT 3 LARGE LEEKS
INTO SLICES (INCLUDE THE
GREEN PARTS!)

SIMMER THE LEEKS IN
BUTTER, THYME & VERMOUTH.

FORM LAYERS:
→ LEEKS, WHITE FISH
→ CHEESE, LEEKS, FISH ETC.
→ POUR HEAVY CREAM
→ OVER, COVER WITH
MASHED POTATOES &
CHEESE → BAKE!

AND BE
HAPPY

There are a few vegetables that improve after braising for a long time. As far as I'm concerned, leeks deserve the number-one spot. The French have known this since forever and serve leeks on their own as a starter called *poireaux vinaigrette*. The soft-braised leeks are served in big chunks—either warm or cold—and covered in a sharp, fresh mustard vinaigrette. This fish pie also almost brings me to tears; the English often make it with spinach, but a pile of those soft-braised leeks makes it so consoling that you'll forget about all your worries from last week.

FiSH PiE WiTH STEAMED LEEKS

Boil the potatoes in salted water, drain, let the steam evaporate, and mash. Add 3½ tablespoons (50 g) of the butter, ¾ cup (75 g) of the Parmesan, a splash of the cream, and salt and pepper to taste, stirring until the puree is smooth and well seasoned.

In a large saucepan, sauté the leeks with the thyme in the remaining butter for about 20 minutes until soft, douse with the vermouth, let evaporate, and season the leeks with salt and pepper.

Preheat the oven to 350°F (180°C).

Grease a baking dish. Arrange layers of the leeks and cod in the dish, sprinkling each layer with some grated cheese and paprika, but also keep some cheese and paprika aside for the top.

Pour the cream over the dish. Cover the dish with the mashed potatoes and sprinkle with the remaining bit of both kinds of cheese, a pinch of paprika, and black pepper. Place the dish on an baking sheet to catch any overflow. Bake the fish pie for 35 to 40 minutes, until nicely golden brown, and serve.

serves 4

2 pounds 3 ounces (1 kg) potatoes, peeled

5 tablespoons (75 g) butter, plus extra

1 cup (100 g) Parmesan cheese, grated

1⅔ cups (400 ml) heavy cream

Sea salt and freshly ground black pepper

3 big leeks, sliced and rinsed

1 tablespoon fresh thyme leaves

Splash of dry vermouth or white wine

1 pound 2 ounces (500 g) cod, diced

1¼ cups (125 g) aged cheese, such as Cheddar, grated

1 teaspoon smoked paprika

SPICED MACKEREL, PAGE 109

SALMON, FENNEL & LEMON WITH SPINACH MISO-MAYO, PAGE 95

BAKING

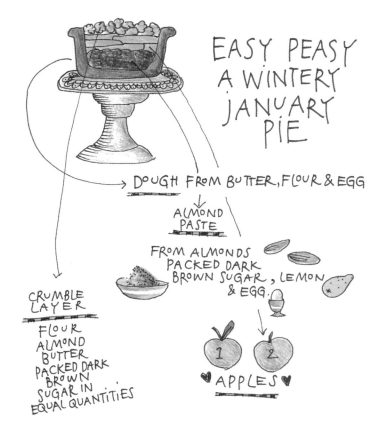

EASY PEASY
A WINTERY
JANUARY
PIE

DOUGH FROM BUTTER, FLOUR & EGG

ALMOND
PASTE

FROM ALMONDS
PACKED DARK
BROWN SUGAR, LEMON
& EGG.

CRUMBLE
LAYER

FLOUR
ALMOND
BUTTER
PACKED DARK
BROWN
SUGAR IN
EQUAL QUANTITIES

1   2

♥ APPLES ♥

I believe that January can be a lovely month. Look, if we keep saying that it's such a gloomy time, at some point everybody will start believing it. I prefer to do the opposite. I went on a gorgeous walk through the fog with our dog. We returned home. I made tea and baked this pie. Fortunately, some friends came over so we could eat it together. Wine was served and no one was in a rush to go home. You see: January can be terribly cozy.

APPLE ALMOND CRUMBLE

Make the dough: Rub the butter together with the flour into a mixture that resembles coarse crumbs. Add the salt and egg and swiftly combine into a firm dough. If it turns a bit too dry, add a drop of ice-cold water. Wrap in plastic and let rest in the refrigerator for 30 minutes to 1 hour.

Roll the dough out into a round that fits a greased 8½- or 9-inch (22 cm) springform pan or a square one of the same size. Pop in the freezer for 30 minutes.

Preheat the oven to 350°F (180°C).

Prebake the frozen pie shell for 15 minutes.

Make the filling: Grind the almonds with the brown sugar, egg, and lemon juice and zest into a smooth paste in a food processor. Spread onto the piecrust and place the apple slices on top.

Make the crumble dough by combining all the ingredients, rubbing them together with cool hands. Sprinkle onto the pie.

Bake for 35 minutes, or until golden brown. Serve with a runny custard or crème fraîche.

serves 6 to 8

FOR THE DOUGH

7 tablespoons (100 g) cold butter

1½ cups (200 g) all-purpose flour

Pinch of sea salt

1 egg

Ice-cold water, if needed

FOR THE FILLING

Scant ¾ cup (100 g) almonds (or almond flour)

Scant ½ cup (100 g) packed dark brown sugar

1 egg

Juice and grated zest of 1 lemon

2 Granny Smith apples, thinly sliced

FOR THE CRUMBLE

6 tablespoons (50 g) all-purpose flour

6 tablespoons (50 g) almond flour

4 tablespoons (50 g) packed dark brown sugar

COMBINE NUT BUTTER, SUGAR, SALT, BUTTER & SELF RISING FLOUR

CHOP THE DARK CHOCOLATE INTO SMALL CHUNKS & COMBINE

WITH AN ICE-CREAM SCOOP, CREATE LITTLE BALLS OF DOUGH ON THE BAKING SHEET

AND BAKE!

2017 was the year of the nut butters. I don't know about you, but I felt I was being bombarded by them. There were some pretty tasty jars among them, but with all due respect, sometimes it's a matter of plain overkill. If you have children this problem is easily solved; you can always offload a jar or two to them, but, well, I'm not in that position. I'm also not much of a peanut butter sandwich kind of person myself, and you can only make satay sauce so often. In short, I was stuck with a shelf full of jars.

So using the butters for baking it was. My first two attempts to bake cookies without flour or dairy went straight into the trashcan. Too bad, but it did clean out my shelf even faster. The next version made this book, and includes regular flour, butter, and an egg. And chocolate, of course, because that truly makes these cookies delicious.

MAKES ABOUT 16 COOKIES

7 tablespoons (100 g) butter, melted

2 cups (250 g) self-rising flour

½ cup (125 g) chocolate hazelnut butter (or 115 g any other nut butter plus 1 tablespoon cocoa powder)

1 egg

2½ ounces (70 g) dark chocolate, chopped into chunks

NUT BUTTER CHOCOLATE CHIP COOKIES

Preheat the oven to 350°F (180°C).

Combine all the ingredients except for the chocolate chunks into a smooth, even mixture. A stand mixer works best, but be careful not to mix for too long or your cookies will turn out thin and chewy instead of crispy. Fold in the chocolate chunks with a metal spoon.

Line one or two baking sheets with parchment paper and use an ice cream scoop or two spoons to form mounds of dough, slightly larger in size than a walnut. Arrange them on the pans a little spaced apart; they will spread slightly. Bake for 12 to 13 minutes, until golden and cooked, the center just set. Let cool completely on a rack.

WHISK THE BUTTER
AND SUGAR UNTIL
LIGHT & AIRY.
ADD THE EGGS
ONE BY ONE

STIR IN
THE THICK
YOGURT.

FOLD IN
THE FLOUR,
CORN STARCH & SALT.

DIVIDE THE BATTER IN 2:

1 MIX 2

ONE HALF
WITH COCOA

ONE. HALF
WITH
PANDAN PASTE

COMBINE
THESE BATTERS
IN A
TURBAN MOLD.

I've been cooking a lot of Indonesian food for some time now. I've lived in the Dutch city of The Hague for years, and that's where I learned how to cook. To the people of The Hague, Indonesian food is what bagels are to New Yorkers: a basic life necessity. A Dutch-Indonesian friend once gave me the tip to use pandan paste for a typical Indonesian dessert. I had always been a little wary of this ingredient because of its neon green color. But the sweet aroma and flavor were so exquisite that I decided to look past that weird color and began to experiment by adding pandan to all sorts of recipes. Pandan paste is made from concentrated pandan leaves, a rather large spear-shaped leaf from a plant native to Asia. It smells like a mix of warm, buttery macadamias and vanilla. According to Nigella Lawson, pandan is the new matcha. Others claim it's the new avocado. Anyway, just quickly bake this cake so you'll remain a step ahead of the hipster crowd.

serves 6 to 8

Make sure all the ingredients are at room temperature.

Baking spray

1 cup (225 g) butter

1 cup plus 2 tablespoons (225 g) sugar

4 eggs

¾ cup plus 1 tablespoon (200 ml) plain yogurt

1¾ cups (225 g) self-rising flour

6 tablespoons (50 g) cornstarch

¼ teaspoon salt

3 tablespoons cocoa powder

1½ teaspoons (10 g) pandan paste (not extract; buy at Asian market or online)

CHOCO-PANDAN-YOGURT MARBLE BUNDT CAKE

Preheat the oven to 350°F (180°C).

Grease a 9½-inch (24 cm) Bundt pan with baking spray. Beat the butter and sugar until fluffy. Add the eggs one by one. Stir in the yogurt. Mix the flour, cornstarch, and salt and fold into the batter.

Divide the batter into two portions. Stir the cocoa powder into one portion until it's evenly brown. Stir the pandan paste into the other.

Dollop spoonfuls of the two batters into the prepared pan and gently streak them together with a spatula. The batter should just about be mixed but you should still be able to clearly distinguish the two colors.

Bake for 40 to 50 minutes, until a skewer inserted in the center comes out clean. Let stand for 5 minutes, then carefully turn the cake out onto a platter.

DISSOLVE YEAST IN LUKEWARM MILK AND LET STAND UNTIL IT'S FOAMING.

REMOVE → PITS!

WHILE YOU WAIT, QUARTER THE PLUMS.

MAKE A NICE DOUGH FROM FLOUR, SALT, BUTTER, A PINCH OF SUGAR & 1 EGG YOLK.

LET RISE

ROLL OUT

ARRANGE THE DOUGH SLAB IN A TART PAN. FILL UP THE TART WITH PLUMS. SPRINKLE WITH SUGAR → BAKE!

A little while ago it was Carnaval. Now, I'm not the type to dance her way from pub to pub in the Dutch South, but I did have some guests over during *vastelaovend* (the eve of Lent). And because my parents are from the southern province of Limburg I did pick up a thing or two in my youth. I decided to cook a large pot of *zoervleis* (meat stew). My father used to make this dark brown sweet-and-sour stew the traditional way—with horse meat—but I used beef instead. Thank god my stew turned out to be just as succulent as the *zoervleis* I remember. I followed good Limburgian tradition and fried a large batch of French fries in tallow, whipped up a homemade mayo, and peeled all the apples for the applesauce myself. For dessert, I baked the traditional pie from the Dutch south: a *vlaai*. I was delighted to find tiny ripe plums in the supermarket and fashioned a fresh little tart with them to finish off this perfect little dinner party.

makes 1 pie; serves 6 (in the southern provinces of the Netherlands) or 8 (anywhere else)

2¼ teaspoons (1 envelope/7 g) instant yeast

7 tablespoons (100 ml) lukewarm milk, plus extra if needed

2⅓ cups (300 g) all-purpose flour, plus extra

Pinch of sea salt

3½ tablespoons (50 g) butter, at room temperature

3 tablespoons superfine granulated sugar, plus extra for sprinkling

1 egg yolk

2 pounds 3 ounces (1 kg) small ripe plums, quartered

Confectioners' sugar, for dusting

PLUM VLAAI

Dissolve the yeast in the lukewarm milk. Sift the flour along with the salt into a bowl. Then add the butter, superfine sugar, and egg yolk. Form an indentation in the center and pour in the yeast mixture. Stir until all the flour has been absorbed and use your flour-dusted hands to knead for 10 minutes, until the dough is supple, adding some extra flour or milk if needed. Let the dough rise for 1 hour in a covered bowl.

Roll out into a round the size of a pie pan (11 to 12 inches/ 28 to 30 cm). Grease the pan, then press the dough into the pan, neatly trim the edges, and poke a few holes in the bottom using a fork.

While the dough rests, preheat the oven to 400°F (200°C).

Arrange the plums, skin side down, in circles in the pan. Lightly sprinkle with superfine sugar. Bake for 35 to 45 minutes, until the plums are cooked but still hold their shape and the edges just start to burn. Rotate the pan halfway through the cooking time so the pie browns evenly. Dust with confectioners' sugar and serve warm.

FIRST

MAKE HANGOP
FROM THICK
GREEK YOGURT.

→ DELICIOUS! ←

WHIP WITH BUTTER →,
CLEMENTINE ZEST,
VANILLA &
CONFECTIONERS' SUGAR.

SECOND

BAKE A CAKE FROM THOSE
SAME INGREDIENTS,
PLUS EGG & FLOUR.

COVER THE CAKE
WITH THE YOGURT GLAZE &
DECORATE WITH CLEMENTINE
SLICES

AMEN

Yes, spring has sprung in fruit land. The clementines are running out or aren't as tasty as before. Sometime around mid-March we'll be eating the last ones, and that'll be it until next October. In a couple of months the first strawberries will slowly begin to appear, but first we must quickly clean out our fruit bowl. With a clementine cake, of course, because Van Boven still had a bowl of them and her mother stopped by for dinner. (Psst! You can also make this cake with oranges, just use half an orange for each clementine. Just as delicious!)

CLEMENTINE YOGURT CAKE

First make the yogurt cream: Pour the yogurt into a dish-cloth placed over a strainer over a bowl. Let strain for at least 4 hours in the fridge.

Spoon the strained yogurt into a mixing bowl and add the butter, clementine zest, vanilla, and salt. Stir in the confectioners' sugar and whisk into a fluffy cream. Refrigerate.

Make the cake crust: Preheat the oven to 350°F (170°C). Grease an 8-inch (20 cm) springform pan or regular round cake pan and line the bottom with parchment paper.

Sift the flour, sugar, baking powder, and the salt into a bowl.

In another bowl, mix the yogurt, oil, clementine zest and juice, egg, and vanilla. Pour the yogurt mixture in with the dry ingredients and swiftly combine into an even, smooth batter.

Pour into the springform pan and bake until golden brown, 25 to 30 minutes. Let cool on a rack for 5 minutes, then remove from the pan, peel off the parchment, and let cool completely.

Spread the cake with the yogurt cream and decorate with the clementine slices. Serve.

makes 1 cake

FOR THE YOGURT CREAM

¾ cup plus 1 tablespoon (200 ml) plain Greek yogurt

2 tablespoons butter, at room temperature

Grated zest of 1 clementine

1 teaspoon vanilla extract

Pinch of sea salt

¾ cup (75 g) sifted confectioners' sugar

FOR THE CAKE CRUST

1 cup (125 g) all-purpose flour

½ cup (100 g) sugar

1 teaspoon baking powder

Pinch of sea salt

¾ cup plus 1 tablespoon (200 ml) plain Greek yogurt

3½ tablespoons (50 ml) vegetable oil

Juice and grated zest of 1 clementine

1 egg

½ teaspoon vanilla extract

2 to 3 clementines, peeled and sliced

Joanna's
TEA COOKIES

MIX :
FLOUR,
BAKING SODA
DARK BROWN SUGAR
ROLLED OATS +
A PINCH OF SALT.

FEEL FREE TO ADD A
FLAVOR : ... JOANNA
S U G G E S T S :

GRATED
LEMON ZEST
OR GINGER

ORANGE
ZEST.

MELT
BUTTER
WITH 1 TBSP.
MILK &
GOLDEN SYRUP.

COMBINE
EVERYTHING
SHAPE INTO
FLAT COOKIES.

BAKE UNTIL
CRUNCHY

Recently I was looking for an old recipe for a dish my mother would often make for us. I called her to ask whether she still had it somewhere, and she diligently dug up her folders of recipes that her own mother had given her when she emigrated to Ireland in the late '60s. This archive is a valuable resource in itself, but she wasn't able to quickly locate the recipe we were looking for. An hour or so later, she sent me a picture of a handwritten recipe for the Irish cookies that her friend Joanna would bake for my birthday every year. Reading it—it had the dubious title "Nig Nogs"—immediately evoked the way the cookies used to taste, and as I'm typing this recipe for you I'm holding one of them between my teeth. Just as crunchy and delicious as I remembered them to be.

JoANNA'S BiRTHDAY TEA CooKiES

Preheat the oven to 300°F (150°C).

Using a whisk, combine the flour, baking soda, salt, brown sugar, oats, lemon zest, and ginger in a large bowl until everything is thoroughly mixed.

Melt the butter along with the milk and golden syrup in a saucepan over medium heat. Make a well in the flour mixture and pour in the melted butter mixture. Using a wooden spoon, stir until everything is combined. If stirring becomes difficult, continue kneading the dough with clean hands for a short while.

Roll into fifteen balls. I use an ice cream scoop so all of them are the same size, which looks very professional.

Space the balls, somewhat flattened, on a parchment paper–lined baking sheet and bake for 25 minutes. Let rest on the pan for 3 minutes, then allow to further cool on a wire rack.

makes 15

¾ cup plus 1 tablespoon (100 g) all-purpose flour

½ teaspoon baking soda

Pinch of sea salt

Scant ½ cup (100 g) packed dark brown sugar

1 cup plus 1 tablespoon (100 g) quick-cooking rolled oats

Grated zest of 1 lemon

½ tablespoon ground ginger

7 tablespoons (100 g) butter

1 tablespoon milk

1 tablespoon golden syrup

PEEL APPLES.
COOK THEM WITH
A SPLASH OF WATER
INTO A COMPOTE.
THEN LET COOL.

WHIP BUTTER & SUGAR
UNTIL AIRY.
ADD THE EGGS 1 BY 1.

STIR IN
THE   LEMON
             ZEST

AND 1 DROP
ALMOND OIL.

THEN FOLD
  IN THE MEAL
  & FLOUR.

MAKE LAYERS:
BATTER, APPLE COMPOTE, BATTER
DECORATE WITH A WHOLE ALMONDS.
BAKE UNTIL GOLDEN BROWN!

PURE
MAGIC

PURE
ALM

There are two kinds of almond oil: sweet and bitter. You'll find the sweet variety everywhere: in energy bars, as a garnish, or in almond paste. The bitter one is harder to find in stores and, if you do, it's usually in the form of an almond extract or oil—as flavor enhancer in gourmet marzipan, for example. With sweet almond oil you can make your violin or your baby's botrtom shine. One drop of the bitter almond oil will render your salad dressing otherworldly, your cakes or pastry chef level, and your walnut or hazelnut ice cream will never be the same without it. Raw bitter almonds do contain cyanide, which *can* cause nasty health effects, but one drop of bitter almond oil is harmless. I've been keeping a minuscule bottle of it in my drawer for about two hundred years. That's how little I've used of it. Not because I'm afraid, but because I don't need more; it's that concentrated. It's one of my favorite flavor makers and soon it will be one of yours, too; buy some and bake this cake.

makes 1 cake

12¼ ounces (350 g) Jonagold apples, peeled, cored, and cubed

14 tablespoons (200 g) butter, at room temperature

1 cup (200 g) sugar

3 large eggs

1 or 2 drops pure bitter almond extract

Grated zest of 1 lemon

1½ cups (200 g) all-purpose flour

2 teaspoons baking powder

Pinch of sea salt

¾ cup plus 2 tablespoons (100 g) almond flour

Generous ⅓ cup (50 g) blanched almonds

ALMOND APPLE CAKE

Cook the apple cubes in a saucepan with a splash of water for 15 minutes, stirring now and then. Let the compote cool.

Preheat the oven to 350°F (180°C). Butter an 8½- to 9½-inch (22 to 24 cm) springform pan.

Cream the butter and sugar until fluffy. Add the eggs one by one. Whisk in the almond extract and lemon zest. Sift the flour, baking powder, and salt over the butter mixture and fold in the almond flour with a spatula.

Spread half of the batter onto the bottom of the springform pan. Distribute the apple compote on top and use two wet spoons to scoop the remaining batter onto the compote. It doesn't have to be perfectly even. The oven will fix it later. Sprinkle with the blanched almonds.

Bake the cake for 45 to 50 minutes, until golden brown. Remove the springform pan after 5 minutes and leave the cake to cool slightly on a wire rack before slicing it.

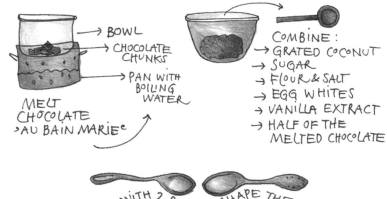

→ BOWL

→ CHOCOLATE
   CHUNKS

→ PAN WITH
   BOILING
   WATER

MELT
CHOCOLATE
"AU BAIN MARIE"

COMBINE:
→ GRATED COCONUT
→ SUGAR
→ FLOUR & SALT
→ EGG WHITES
→ VANILLA EXTRACT
→ HALF OF THE
   MELTED CHOCOLATE

WITH 2 SPOONS, SHAPE THE
DOUGH INTO LITTLE HALF EGGS.
→ SPACE THESE OUT ON THE
   BAKING SHEET.

WHISK THE REST OF THE
CHOCOLATE TOGETHER
WITH BUTTER &
CONFECTIONERS SUGAR
INTO A CREME.
AND VANILLA EXTRACT

USE IT AS GLUE
FOR THE EGG
HALVES → TO
MAKE THEM
W H O L E ♥

You have to imagine that back in the day, before we made them change their biological calendars for our own convenience, chickens used to lay eggs only in the spring instead of year-round. Traditionally Catholics would save up the eggs their chickens began to lay in mid-March, because during Lent they had to abstain from meat, dairy, and other luxuries like chocolate and sugar. Afterward the eggs would be used for a lavish Easter breakfast that signaled the end of the fasting period.

As a child, I briefly lived in the southern Dutch province of Limburg, where these traditions are still very much alive. I too had a "Lent tin" in which I saved up all my candy for Easter, when I could wolf it all down. This is where chocolate Easter eggs come from; they represented a double luxury (because: egg *and* chocolate) that you were finally allowed to enjoy again. In a sense, the Catholic Easter breakfast is not unlike the Islamic Eid al-Fitr tradition—a feast-meal to celebrate the end of fasting.

makes 12

3½ ounces (100 g) dark chocolate, chopped

2½ cups (200 g) desiccated coconut

1 cup (200 g) granulated sugar

6 tablespoons (50 g) all-purpose flour

Pinch of sea salt

3 egg whites

2 teaspoons vanilla extract

7 tablespoons (100 g) butter, at room temperature

1½ cups (150 g) sifted confectioners' sugar, plus extra for dusting

CHOCOLATE EASTER EGGS DELUXE

Preheat the oven to 340°F (170°C). Line a baking sheet with parchment paper.

Melt the chocolate *au bain-marie* (in a double boiler); let cool slightly. Combine the coconut, granulated sugar, flour, and salt. Stir in the egg whites and half of the vanilla, thoroughly mixing everything into an even, thick batter. Pour in half of the melted chocolate and mix well once more. Using two tablespoons, shape twenty-four "egg halves" from the batter and place them on the prepared baking sheet.

Bake for about 15 minutes, until just about done; they will still be a little soft in the middle. Let cool completely.

Whip the butter, confectioners' sugar, the rest of the melted chocolate, and the remaining vanilla together until wonderfully fluffy. Smear a dab of this cream on the flat side of half of the macaroons. Complete your "eggs" by pressing the other halves on top. Dust with confectioners' sugar.

LEMON PEEL

MILK

SUGAR

CARDAMOM

& VANILLA EXTRACT

LET GENTLY STEEP

ADD SEMOLINA & COOK INTO A PORRIDGE

STIR IN 2 EGG YOLKS

& WHIPPED EGG WHITE

POUR INTO GREASE MUFFIN TINS & BAKE!

One Sunday afternoon my chomp chums, Janneke Vreugden-hil and Jacques Hermus, and I hosted a boisterous charity used-cookbooks sale at Staal, a restaurant in the city of Haarlem. Jacques skillfully auctioned off the better items among the offerings that had been brought in by, among other benefactors, the three of us. I became the lucky owner of a pretty little book from 1924 titled *Zelfstandig Koken* (*The Independent Cook*), which was aimed at girls who had graduated from homemaking school. I love these types of publications because they offer a peek into our food history. Sometimes I cannot help but laugh; beef tenderloin was cooked until gray. Other recipes, however, are nice and simple and surprisingly tasty even today. Do you remember my recipe for Gnocchi alla Romana from February on page 25? This is basically a sweet and fluffier take on that dish. I tweaked it somewhat for you and like to serve it with my Baked Apple with Blueberries recipe, *also* from the oven (page 153), because the original recipe calls for rhubarb and early April is a bit too soon for that. P.S.: Boys may prepare this as well.

serves 8

4½ cups (1 L) milk

⅓ cup (60 g) sugar

1 teaspoon vanilla extract, a piece of lemon peel, and/or 4 lightly crushed cardamom pods

½ cup plus 1 tablespoon (100 g) semolina

2 eggs, separated

Pinch of sea salt

1924-STYLE BAKED SEMOLINA PUDDINGS

Preheat the oven to 325°F (160°C).

Bring the milk, sugar, vanilla, lemon zest, and cardamom pods to a boil and reduce the heat to medium. Pour in the semolina and, while stirring, cook until reduced to a thick porridge, about 5 minutes. Remove from the heat and beat in the egg yolks.

Once it has cooled somewhat, remove the lemon peel and cardamom pods (if you used them) from the porridge. Beat the egg whites and salt until stiff. Fold the egg foam into the semolina porridge and carefully pour the mixture into a greased oven dish or several smaller greased ramekins.

Bake for about 30 minutes, until risen and nicely golden brown. Serve with Baked Apples with Blueberries, if desired.

OOH SO GOOD,
AS DESSERT
OR BREAKFAST:

SMALL APPLES
FILLED WITH
BLUEBERRY,
ALMOND FLOUR,
PINCH OF SUGAR,
CARDAMOM,
VANILLA
&
LEMON JUICE.

Although spring has already begun, it'll still be some time until the first true spring crops. On Facebook and in newsletters, recipes for rhubarb are popping up, but I haven't seen any rhubarb in the supermarket yet. Still a little too soon. The rhubarb in my garden is making strides, but for now I'll make do with another zesty fruit dessert from the oven. This apple dish is surprisingly easy to make, and the swift mixture of almond flour and sugar lends a hint of a French apple pie with frangipane. What an invention! The soft almond flavor in combination with the tart apple also works really well with the semolina pudding from the previous recipe. Instead of dessert, you can serve this dish for breakfast, by the way, just so you know. A versatile snack, which kids no doubt will also love to make.

serves 4

4 tart apples, peeled

Juice of ½ lemon

Handful of blueberries

½ teaspoon ground cardamom

1 teaspoon vanilla extract

1 glass of juice

1½ tablespoons sugar

4 tablespoons (30 g) almond flour

BAKED APPLES WITH BLUEBERRIES

Preheat the oven to 350°F (180°C).

Hollow out the apples with an apple corer, widening the hole somewhat using a sharp knife. Sprinkle the apples with lemon juice and place in an oven dish.

Combine all the remaining ingredients and fill the holes of the apples with the mixture. To make all of the filling fit, just heap it on. Pour the cider around the apples and carefully slide the dish into the oven.

Bake for about 35 minutes, until the apples are tender. Halfway through the cooking time, baste the apples with the sauce from the dish.

Serve as they are, along with ice cream, sour cream, yogurt, or with those delicious baked semolina puddings from the previous page.

CHOP YOUR RHUBARB

INTO SMALLER CHUNKS

AND CUT THOSE IN HALF

FIT ALL PIECES
THE LONG ONES AND
THE SHORTER ONES
IN A SUGAR-COATED
BAKING PAN.

C O V E R

WITH A DOUGH
BLANKET.

BAKE &
INVERT

★

There are rhubarb haters and rhubarb lovers. I consider myself a member of the latter group. As with white asparagus, I really look forward to the moment their season begins, and this year I have them in my own garden for the first time. And not just that: It was the first plant I bought for my new garden. Rhubarb is a member of the Polygonaceae family, and only certain parts of the plants are edible: the stems, of course, *and* the flower buds. You throw out the leaves. Later in the season the oxalate content makes them increasingly acidic, therefore—like with asparagus—we leave them alone after St. John's Day (sometime around June 21 to 24) so they can regain their strength to make us happy again with a new harvest next season. But for now, it's all about taking advantage of the current crop.

makes 1 tart

1 pound 7 ounces (650 g) rhubarb

Generous ⅓ cup (75 g) sugar

1 vanilla bean

Grated zest of 1 orange

Some flour

5 small sheets (8 ounces [225 g] total) puff pastry

RHUBARB TATIN

Preheat the oven to 400°F (200°C). Grease an 8½-inch (22 cm) pie pan.

Cut the rhubarb into 2¾-inch (7 cm) pieces, then cut half of those in half once more.

Sprinkle two-thirds of the sugar and two-thirds of the orange zest into the pie pan. Halve the vanilla bean and scrape out the seeds. Sprinkle them over the sugar and place the bean on top. Arrange the longer rhubarb pieces clockwise around it. Fill up the gaps by placing the shorter pieces in between and in the middle, making sure that everything is covered by a single, even layer of rhubarb. Sprinkle with the rest of the sugar and zest.

On a flour-dusted counter, roll out the puff pastry sheets into one slab that nicely fits the pie pan. Using the apple corer, make a hole in the middle to allow the steam to escape. Fit the dough slab over the layer of rhubarb. Tuck it in nice and tight and, using a fork, poke holes everywhere.

Bake the tart for 30 minutes. Let rest briefly, then turn it out onto a plate. Serve straightaway.

MAKE CARROT CAKE-MUESLI BARS
WHETHER YOU'RE A DUTCH ROYALIST
OR NOT.

WHIP BUTTER
& SUGAR UNTIL
AIRY, WHIP IN
THE ●● EGGS
+ VANILLA

GRATE CARROTS OF
EVERY COLOR.

COMBINE WHOLE-WHEAT FLOUR
WITH BAKING POWDER, PINCH OF SALT,
& MUESLI WITH THE BATTER & BAKE!

WHIP CREAM
CHEESE &
CONFECTIONERS'
SUGAR → ICE
THE CAKE WITH IT.
CUT INTO
WEDGES.

There's a story claiming that carrots owe their orange color to the Dutch royal family of Oranje-Nassau. I can't confirm this because I wasn't born yet, but what I do know is that carrots haven't always been orange. The precursors of our current carrots were brought over from Iran by the Dutch East India Company VOC in the seventeenth century. In the Netherlands, these were crossbred until they developed a tint that may have had something to do with the Dutch national color (but there's no real proof for that). However, those picturesque purple and white rainbow carrots that I've been sowing in my garden—and that can be bought everywhere these days—probably better resemble the first carrots, which were around long before our contemporary orange root vegetable. Orange carrots do contain more beta carotene—which our body transforms into vitamin A—than their white and purple brothers, though. Use this to your advantage, I'd say.

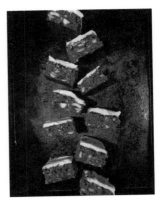

ROYAL CARROT CAKE MUESLI BARS

Preheat the oven to 350°F (180°C). Grease a 7 by 11-inch (18 by 28 cm) brownie pan. Line the bottom with parchment paper, leave the edges hanging over the sides. Grease the paper as well.

Cream the butter and brown sugar until fluffy. One by one, beat in the eggs. Beat in the vanilla.

Combine the flour, baking powder, salt, carrots, and muesli mixture and fold into the egg mixture with a spatula.

Spoon into the brownie pan, smooth the top, and bake for about 35 minutes. The center should be just about solidified, no longer gelatinous. Let cool completely. Lift out with the overhanging parchment paper.

Make the topping: Whip the cream cheese with the confectioners' sugar until fluffy, then spread on top of the cake. Slice into bars and serve.

makes 9 or 12 pieces

6 tablespoons (85 g) butter, at room temperature, plus extra for greasing

1 cup (200 g) lightly packed dark brown sugar

2 eggs

1 tablespoon vanilla extract

1 cup (125 g) whole-wheat flour

1½ teaspoons baking powder

½ teaspoon salt

2¼ cups (250 g) grated carrots

1¼ cups (150 g) mixture of muesli or granola, seeds, chopped nuts and dried fruits

FOR THE TOPPING

7 ounces (200 g) cream cheese, at room temperature

11 tablespoons (160 g) confectioners' sugar

COMBINE BUTTER, EGGS, SUGAR, FLOUR, MILK & VANILLA SUGAR AT ONCE: HOPS! INTO A SMOOTH BATTER

POUR INTO A SPRINGFORM AND BAKE.

WHIP HEAVY CREAM & CRÈME FRAÎCHE

LOOK: A CLASSIC VICTORIA SPONGE CAKE HAS MANY LAYERS...

JAM!

CLEAN THE STRAW-BERRIES!

SMEAR IT ALL IN BETWEEN.

BUT I LEFT MINE OPEN ONE FOR MY MUM ♥ & ONE FOR ME

Yesssss! There they were, beaming in my direction at the fruit stall; shiny, firm, red Dutch strawberries. I slid a fat container full of them into a brown paper bag and on my way home I contemplated what to make with them. My mind was a whirlwind and whispering all sorts of outrageous ideas into my ears, but I settled on a good old Victoria sponge cake anyway. The English know best what to do with strawberries and cream. And no, this isn't the most original recipe from my repertoire; but oh well, it just happens to be incredibly delicious and on Mother's Day it will delight any mum. A Victoria sponge really is a sandwich cake; the filling goes in the middle. But I left it open-faced; that way I suddenly had two cakes: one for my mother and one for myself.

makes 2 open-faced cakes (or 1 sandwiched)

FOR THE CAKE

1 cup (225 g) butter, at room temperature

4 eggs

1 cup (225 g) packed light brown sugar

2 cups plus 6 tablespoons (300 g) self-rising flour

4 tablespoons (60 ml) milk

1 teaspoon vanilla extract

FOR THE FILLING (OR TOPPING)

½ (13-ounce/370 g) jar strawberry jam

¾ cup plus 1 tablespoon (200 ml) heavy cream

½ cup (125 ml) crème fraîche

10½ ounces (300 g) strawberries, cleaned, large ones cut into smaller pieces

Confectioners' sugar and, if you like, some woodruff (or sweet bedstraw) for garnish

VICTORIA SPONGE

Make the cake: Preheat the oven to 350°F (180°C). Grease a 9½-inch (24 cm) springform pan.

Using a hand mixer, combine all ingredients for the cake into a smooth batter.

Pour into the springform pan and bake for about 35 minutes, until the cake bounces back when you gently press down on it with your fingertips. Let cool for 5 minutes, then remove the springform. Allow to thoroughly cool on a rack.

Halve the cake widthwise. Spread with the jam. Whip the heavy cream with the crème fraîche and spoon it on top. Arrange the strawberries on top and sprinkle with confectioners' sugar and the flowers of your woodruff, if you choose. Give one cake to your mother (or a charming neighbor).

FROM BREAD TO
PARFAIT IN JUST
A FEW STEPS.

NEVER THROW OUT OLD BREAD!
BAKE THE CRUMBS ALL
CRUNCHY WITH BROWN
SUGAR

MIX
WITH
CUSTARD

+

WHIPPED
EGG WHITE

POUR INTO A LOAF TIN
FREEZE.
VOILA: PARFAIT!

Don't give me that look! This seriously is a wonderfully delicious Irish dessert. The Irish never throw out food. Stale soda bread is often used for making ice cream and this recipe happens to be one of my favorites. Just try it sometime. The bliss of those crunchy chunks (and a splash of Irish whiskey!) will knock you off your feet. I like to use my cute little ice cream maker, but I'm aware that not everyone has one. Therefore, I tweaked the recipe so that anyone with a freezer can make this fluffy parfait, either one large one or lots of small ones. See: even the ice cream is coming out of Van Boven's oven.

BROWN BREAD PARFAIT

Preheat the oven to 400°F (200°C).

In a food processor, pulse the bread along with the brown sugar and a pinch of salt into crumbs. Spread on a parchment paper–lined baking sheet. Bake for 10 minutes, until the sugar has caramelized. Set aside to cool.

Thoroughly beat the egg yolks and granulated sugar until light yellow and very frothy. In a saucepan, bring the cream and vanilla to just below a boil and, while whisking continuously, slowly pour it into the egg mixture. Pour everything back into the saucepan and reheat until it thickens and sticks to the back of your spoon. Remove from the heat and let it cool slightly. Stir the buttermilk and whiskey, if using, into the custard.

Beat the egg whites and a pinch of salt until stiff. Fold into the custard. Fold in the baked crumbs at the very end.

Line a cake pan with plastic wrap or use multiple smaller cake cups. Pour in the mixture, cover with plastic wrap, and refrigerate until solidified, at least 4 hours.

serves 6 to 8

1 thick slice stale Irish soda bread or dark whole-wheat bread (2½ to 3½ ounces/75 to 100 g)

¼ cup (50 g) lightly packed dark brown sugar

Sea salt

4 eggs, separated

Generous ½ cup (110 g) granulated sugar

¾ cup plus 1 tablespoon (200 ml) heavy cream

1 teaspoon vanilla extract

1¼ cups (300 ml) buttermilk

3 to 4 tablespoons whiskey (optional)

CHERRY CLAVANISH

IT'S BEST TO MACERATE THE CHERRIES

THEY'LL BE NICE & SOFT, WITH SUGAR, KIRSH & —ZEST.

>>> → BUT IT'S NOT MANDATORY! ← <<<
YOU CAN ALSO CONTINUE STRAIGHT AWAY

PLACE THE CHERRIES IN A SINGLE LAYER IN A GREASED TART PAN

IN A GREASED TART PAN!

POUR IN A BATTER MADE OF EGG, MILK, MELTED BUTTER, FLOUR & SUGAR + 1 DROP OF AMAN ALMOND OIL (IF DESIRED)

BAKE UNTIL THE CLAFOUTIS IS JUST SET.

Long ago, a new beau took me to visit his friends. Everyone was nervous—him, because: new girlfriend. And I, because I felt I had to make an impression. Everybody would prepare something for the meal, and I confidently told him that things were in good hands with me. I chopped a lot of fruits: grapes, strawberries, melon, pineapple, and some kiwi to add a bit of green. I made a Prosecco jelly and let it stiffen with the fruits mixed in. At least, that was the plan. Back then, I didn't know that pineapple and kiwi contain an element that stops the solidifying of jelly. Anyway, boyfriend panics: He foresaw an impending defeat with his soggy bowl of fruit salad. I took a deep breath, drained the mess, and searched the kitchen for eggs, milk, and flour. I scooped the fruit salad into a baking dish. Poured batter on top and bam: The vanished jelly had been transformed into clafoutis. The corny pun was a matter of minutes. As was this dessert. Here you have the *real* recipe.

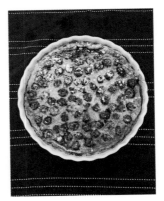

serves 6

1 pound 2 ounces (500 g) cherries, pitted

2 tablespoons plus ⅓ cup (65 g) granulated sugar

3 tablespoons kirsch or brandy

Grated zest of ½ lemon

3 eggs

1¼ cups (300 ml) milk

2 tablespoons butter, melted

3 drops pure bitter almond oil (or almond extract)

½ cup plus 1 tablespoon (75 g) all-purpose flour

Sea salt

Confectioners' sugar, for dusting

CHERRY CLAVANISH

Note: The French don't pit their cherries, but I don't enjoy eating a pie like that. Also, pitted cherries are much safer for your crowns.

Place the cherries in a bowl, spoon in 2 tablespoons of the granulated sugar, the liquor, and lemon zest and let macerate for at least 1 hour.

Preheat the oven to 350°F (180°C). Generously butter a baking dish.

Beat the eggs, milk, butter, and almond oil together.

Combine the flour, the remaining ⅓ cup granulated sugar, and a pinch of salt in a mixing bowl. While whisking, pour in the egg-milk mixture and continue stirring until all lumps have dissolved.

Scoop the cherries and their liquid into the baking dish. Pour in the runny batter and carefully slide the dish into the hot oven. Bake for about 30 minutes, until the egg has just set but still is gelatinous—gelatinous in the good sense of the word, that is. Dust with confectioners' sugar and serve.

BLIND BAKING

PRESS PARCHMENT PAPER NEATLY INTO THE DOUGH-LINED PAN.

FILL THE PARCHMENT PAPER WITH A FAUX FILLING, LIKE DRIED BEANS OR RICE.

AFTER BLIND BAKING, GENTLY REMOVE THE PARCHMENT PAPER WITH THE FAUX FILLING. KEEP IT FOR THE NEXT BAKE → YOU CAN NO LONGER COOK AND EAT YOUR DRIED BEANS OR RICE — BY THE WAY——

One of my good friends, Meike, owns a bakery: Petit Gateau. Whenever we have something to celebrate, we eat heaps of small tarts in every flavor imaginable. Meike learned her trade from a confectioner in Paris. Her tarts are made from the most delicious dough and filled with anything her rich fantasy can conjure up. Once I planned on stealing her secret dough recipe, but now anyone can simply look it up in her book, just like all of her fillings. Below you'll find our collaborative recipe, half mine and the other half from Meike Schaling's book *Kleine Taartjes*. Thanks, Meike!

GRAND GATEAU À LA RHUBARBE

Make the dough: Combine all of the dry ingredients for the dough and swiftly rub in the cold butter. Add as much egg as needed to make a cohesive ball. Sometimes 1 tablespoon is enough. Wrap the dough in plastic and refrigerate for 1 hour.

Make the filling: Puree the strawberries with the sugar in a blender. Beat the mascarpone with the vanilla extract.

Grease an 8½-inch (22 cm) cake pan. Roll out the dough on a flour-dusted counter until it is ⅛ inch (3 mm) thick, press it neatly into the pan, and trim the edges. Store in the fridge for 30 minutes.

Preheat the oven to 340°F (170°C). Fill the dough crust with blind baking weights (for example, a handful of dry beans) and bake for about 30 minutes. Remove the weights and bake for another 7 minutes.

Meanwhile, arrange the rhubarb in a single layer in a baking pan or roasting pan. Drizzle with the strawberry pulp and poach in the oven next to the cake for 25 minutes. Let everything cool.

If the rhubarb is very wet, drain in a sieve. (Save the liquid for stirring into yogurt!) Fill the crust with the mascarpone and top with the strawberry rhubarb. Serve.

serves 6 to 8

FOR THE DOUGH

2½ tablespoons all-purpose flour, plus extra

½ cup (50 g) sifted confectioners' sugar

3 tablespoons almond flour

Pinch of sea salt

5 tablespoons (75 g) cold butter, diced

1 egg, beaten

FOR THE FILLING

1 pound 10 ounces (750 g) strawberries (fresh or frozen)

1 cup minus 2 tablespoons (175 g) granulated sugar

1 cup plus 1 tablespoon (250 ml) mascarpone

1 teaspoon vanilla extract

4 to 5 stalks rhubarb, halved lengthwise and cut into 1½-inch (4 cm) pieces

PLACE A HEAVY
(CAST-IRON) SKILLET
IN THE OVEN.

BLEND EGG-
YOLKS, FLOUR,
SUGAR, VANILLA,
LEMON ZEST,
MILK & NUTMEG
IN A BLENDER

WHIP EGG WHITES
UNTIL STIFF AND
FOLD INTO THE BATTER.

WEAR OVEN MITS!
AND OPEN THE OVEN.
MELT BUTTER
IN THE HOT PAN.

POUR IN
THE BATTER
STRAIGHT AWAY.
DECORATE WITH
FRUIT → BAKE!

I am a big fan of the Dutch baby—a gigantic oven-baked puffed pancake brought to America by immigrants. The name is said to have derived from the Pennsylvania Dutch, who are German Americans, by the way, not Dutch at all. Anyway, there's only a slight difference between the sound of *Deutsch* and *Dutch*, and whoever mispronounced it coined a new term. Personally, I think these look suspiciously like Yorkshire puddings. Very Anglican/British, therefore, the big difference being that when you make Yorkshire pudding, the batter is poured into red-hot cast-iron ramekins or muffin pans greased with animal fat (drippings or gravy), whereas the Dutch baby is baked in a piping-hot cast-iron pan in which butter has melted. In the end, they are all popovers. Americans eat them with confectioners' sugar, the English with their Sunday roast. I whisk the egg whites separately, fold those in, and bake the stone fruit along with the batter. Call it whatever you want.

serves 2 as breakfast or brunch dish

2 tablespoons granulated sugar

1 teaspoon vanilla extract

Grated zest of ½ lemon

3 eggs, separated

½ cup plus 2 tablespoons (150 ml) whole milk

½ cup plus 1 tablespoon (75 g) all-purpose flour

Pinch of freshly grated nutmeg

Pinch of sea salt

3½ tablespoons (50 g) butter

3 whole stone fruits, pitted and cut into wedges

Confectioners' sugar, for sprinkling

HANDY

Ovenproof (cast-iron) skillet or tartine pan

MY KINDA DUTCH BABY WITH STONE FRUIT

Preheat the oven to 435°F (225°C) and place a cast-iron skillet in the middle.

Pulse the plain sugar, vanilla sugar, lemon zest, egg yolks, milk, flour, and nutmeg in a blender until smooth. In a clean bowl, beat the egg whites with the salt until stiff.

Open the oven door and slide a pat of butter into the hot pan. It will melt immediately, so gently sway the pan back and forth (use oven mitts!) to spread the butter all around. Immediately pour the batter into the scorching pan, arrange the slices of fruit on top, and shut the oven.

Bake the pancake until it is puffed and done; about 18 minutes.

Slide onto a large plate, sprinkle with confectioners' sugar, and serve.

ARE YOUR PEACHES STILL HARD?

... USE THEM TO BAKE A TART WITH.

SIFT FLOUR, SALT & BAKING POWDER

WITH CLEAN HANDS KNEAD IN THE BUTTER.

STIR IN THE BROWN SUGAR.

AND 2 BEATEN EGGS PLUS 2 DROPS OF MILK - IF YOU WISH -

PRESS THE DOUGH INTO THE PAN & FILL WITH HALVED HARD PEACHES (OR APRICOTS).

SERVE WITH WHIPPED CREAM!

I really fell for it. At the supermarket, I spotted those beautiful wild peaches. Well, wild, wild . . . I thought, wild. That may have been the case in the past, but now that they are ubiquitous, it's hard to imagine. Last year I used to buy them at the farmers' market; they were juicy, full of flavor, and easy to eat. Their practical shape made them perfect for nibbling away. Long story short, after four days, the ones from the supermarket were still hard. And not that tasty, either. How could you have been so stupid, Van Boven? I thought. Who buys their fruit at the supermarket anyway? Those big stores stick to their delivery times whether the fruits are ripe or not. I decided to bake a pie with them, because when you heat it, fruit will automatically soften. And so it happened. The result was enormously delicious. The perfect solution, as it turned out.

makes 1 pie

2 cups (250 g) all-purpose flour

½ teaspoon baking powder

Pinch of sea salt

12 tablespoons (125 g) butter, at room temperature, cubed

About 9 tablespoons (125 g) lightly packed light brown sugar

2 eggs, beaten

1 to 2 tablespoons milk, heavy cream, or water

6 peaches or apricots, preferably wild

Confectioners' sugar, for sprinkling

1 tablespoon heavy cream or crème fraîche

PEACH SCONE PIE

Into a bowl, sift the flour, baking powder, and salt. With clean, cold fingers, rub in the butter until the mixture resembles coarse crumbs.

Mix in about 6½ tablespoons (90 grams) of the light brown sugar and form a well at the center for the beaten eggs. Pour them in. Swiftly stir everything together into a smooth and supple dough. If it's a bit too dry, add a drop of milk.

Preheat the oven to 350°F (180°C).

Grease an 8½-inch (22 cm) metal baking pan or an enameled one (porcelain or glass aren't suited for this recipe because those materials heat up too slowly). Press the dough into the pan, making sure the edges are high by using a fork. Poke holes into the bottom with a fork or skewer.

Halve the fruits (peaches don't necessarily have to be peeled), remove the pits, and arrange the halves over the dough. Sprinkle with the remaining sugar. Bake the pie for 30 to 40 minutes, until golden brown and done. Sprinkle with confectioners' sugar. Serve with heavy cream or crème fraîche.

PINCH OF SALT

MIX

1¾ CUPS SELF-RISING FLOUR

1 CUP (200 G) SUGAR

WHISK!

4 EGGS

1 CUP (200 G) RICOTTA

1 DROP VANILLA EXTRACT.

ZEST OF ½ LEMON

FOLD IN THE FLOUR MIXTURE.

COVER THE BOTTOM OF A GREASED BAKING PAN WITH YOUR FRESH-PICKED BLACKBERRIES.

POUR THE BATTER ON TOP BAKE FOR A GOOD HALF HOUR

Recently I went on a walk in the Amsterdam park Geuzenbos with city ecologist Geert Timmermans. It's a beautifully wild nature reserve on which he keeps a close eye: "Look over there, brooding common terns! I'm trying my best to keep them here; hopefully their population here will increase." Or he points out the composition of the soil in this reclaimed land, which leads to an ever-changing vegetation: "Look over here, where the soil suddenly turns sandy you find sea buckthorn everywhere." A funny sight at a location devoid of dunes. Everywhere you look, lush and in abundance: blackberries. It has been a good blackberry year. Sometimes they're tiny and dry, but this year—it rained a lot and it was hot—they're big, fat, and juicy. On our way home, we picked a container full of them.

It's not often legal to go foraging in the Netherlands, but picking a small portion of blackberries for personal use at home, for this cake for instance, is permitted. The rest is for the city's wildlife, like the birds that Geert so passionately hopes to keep here.

makes 1 cake

1⅔ cups (200 g) self-rising
   flour

1 cup (200 g) sugar

Pinch of sea salt

4 eggs

1 cup plus 1 tablespoon
   (250 ml) ricotta

1 teaspoon vanilla extract

Grated zest of ½ lemon

7 tablespoons (100 g) butter,
   melted

12¼ ounces (350 g)
   blackberries

BLACKBERRY RICOTTA CAKE

Preheat the oven to 350°F (180°C). Grease an 8½- to 9½-inch (22 to 24 cm) springform pan and line the bottom with a circle of parchment paper cut to fit. Grease the parchment as well.

Combine the flour, sugar, and salt. Beat the eggs with the ricotta, vanilla, and lemon zest. Lastly, beat in the melted butter.

Fold in the flour mixture and stir to make a smooth batter.

Arrange the blackberries over the bottom of the springform pan. Spoon the batter on top and smooth with the back of a wet spoon.

Bake the cake for about 35 minutes, until nicely done. Let it cool slightly on a wire rack, then turn out onto a handsome platter, remove the parchment, and serve.

PEEL A BUNCH OF RIPE PEARS

PROCESS SUGAR & STAR ANISE, COMBINE W. BUTTER & MELT INTO CARAMEL.

PLACE THE PEARHALVES IN THE PIE PAN, CUT SIDE UP

SPRINKLE WITH ALMOND PASTE, COMBINED WITH STAR ANISE & LEMON ZEST.

COVER WITH A BLANKET OF DOUGH AND BAKE!

Years ago, my sister and I gave our mother a pear tree. I believe it was for her birthday. We thought that our mother, an avid gardener, would be very happy with such a present. But no matter how much love and care she devoted to her garden and that little tree, not a single pear appeared. Quite a deception. It became an annual topic of conversation. The tree was growing perfectly well but never bearing any fruits.

Until this fall, when suddenly the tree had seen the light, and she didn't just grow one lonely pear but a big basket full of them. Out of sheer excitement, my mother didn't know what to do with such abundance. So I helped her out in the kitchen. Now my mother finally had pears for her heirs, and baked ones at that. And what a delicious tarte tatin it was.

makes 1 pie

6 large or 8 small ripe pears

Juice and grated zest of
  ½ lemon

5 pieces star anise

3 tablespoons sugar

4 tablespoons (55 g) butter,
  diced

5¼ ounces (150 g) almond
  paste

1 large sheet (half a 17.3-ounce/
  490 g box) all-butter puff
  pastry, rolled out, corners
  rounded

PEAR TATIN WITH STAR ANISE & ALMOND PASTE

Preheat the oven to 400°F (200°C).

Peel the pears, halve them, and, if necessary, remove their harder cores. Toss with the lemon juice.

In a mini food processor or mortar, grind 3 of the star anise and the sugar. Put the mixture with the butter cubes in a shallow 8- to 8½-inch (20 to 22 cm) cake pan. Place in the oven for about 10 minutes, until everything is melted and deep amber.

In the meantime, grind the remaining 2 star anise in the food processor, then pulse in the almond paste and lemon zest. Place the pear halves, cut sides up, in the melted caramel in the cake pan. Sprinkle with the almond paste crumbs.

Cover with a blanket of puff pastry, neatly tucking in the edges. Make a hole in the middle so the steam can escape.

Bake the tarte tatin until golden brown, 30 to 45 minutes, then turn out onto a nice plate almost right away. Serve.

WEIRD JAM

A jar that N° ONE WILL EVER FINISH?

NO WORRIES BAKE A CAKE.

⤷ MAKE DOUGH.

ROLL IT OUT

FIT IT INTO A CAKE PAN

TOP WITH JAM

CUT SHAPES OUT OF THE REMAINING DOUGH, ARRANGE ON TOP.

BAKE!

In the intro to the meatloaf recipe (page 123), I wrote about the remarkable collection of jars with pickled food in my new pantry. I could say the same about jam; my homemade jams, those made by neighbors and friends, the artisanal ones with innovative flavors that I received from producers, together they take up an entire shelf. Suddenly I remembered a tip from my Italian cleaning heroine Maria: Whenever she has unexpected visitors she quickly bakes a crostata filled with a jar of jam, because almost everyone has a jar of jam at home. Same applies to butter and flour. The result: a smart and easy dessert, and one that will please most, especially if you tell them the jam is "homemade by my neighbor!" That way, a simple pie suddenly becomes fascinating.

makes 1 pie

2 cups (250 g) all-purpose flour, plus extra

9 tablespoons (125 g) cold butter, cubed, plus extra for greasing the pan

Pinch of sea salt

Juice of 2 clementines, 1 orange, or 1 lemon (adjust to the type of jam)

1 jar (12¼-ounce/350 g) fig jam or another kind of jam

Granulated or confectioners' sugar, for dusting

CROSTATA WITH FIG JAM

Combine the flour and salt with the butter until you get coarse crumbs; preferably pulse in a food processor: That way the butter stays the coldest. Drop by drop, add just enough clementine juice for the dough to come together. Shape into a flattened ball, wrap in plastic, and let rest in the refrigerator for 1 hour.

Preheat the oven to 400°F (200°C).

On a flour-dusted counter, roll out the dough into a thin slab. Grease a shallow 8½-inch (22 cm) pie pan and press in the dough. Neatly trim the edges. Fill evenly with the jam.

Sweep together all of the dough trimmings, roll out again, and cut out little shapes. Place on top of the filling.

Bake the crostata for 25 to 30 minutes; it should lightly brown. Once it has cooled off, dust the crostata with sugar and serve.

MIX

APPLE CUBES,

LEMON JUICE

RAISINS,

RUM,

GROUND GINGER
CINNAMON
GROUND CLOVES

SALT.

LET STAND FOR 1 HOUR TO 1 NIGHT

COMBINE CINNAMON
WITH SELF-RISING
FLOUR. RUB IN BUTTER
UNTIL IT'S A COARSE
MIXTURE

MIX IN
SUGAR
(DARK BROWN!)
AND
EGGS.
SCOOP 2/3
OF THE APPLE CUBES INTO
THE BATTER. SPOON INTO
A SPRINGFORM PAN.

CLUCK!

SPOON THE REMAINING
APPLE ON TOP.
SPRINKLE CANE SUGAR
OVER IT → FINISH
IN THE OVEN.

Sometimes I receive mail from concerned readers whose pie or cake wasn't done within the cooking time I had indicated. That's very well possible. I can't repeat this often enough, so we'll do a little refreshment course. Ovens vary widely in temperatures, even those from the same brand. Therefore, any cooking times and temperatures mentioned in these recipes should be regarded as reliable suggestions. However, do adjust them to your own oven if necessary. Buy an oven thermometer so you'll know exactly how hot your oven burns. The dial on the outside or front of the oven doesn't indicate the internal temperature, just the desired temperature. For more info about ovens, see page 5 of this book.

To practice, I give you this recipe for a simple but divine apple cake.

APPLE-RUM-RAISIN CAKE

Cube the apples, toss with the lemon juice, raisins, rum, ginger, cinnamon, cloves, and salt and let stand for 1 hour to overnight.

Preheat the oven to 350°F (180°C). Thoroughly grease an 8-inch (20 cm) springform pan.

Make the batter: In a food processor or by hand, combine the cinnamon with the flour. Pulse or cut in the butter until the mixture resembles coarse crumbs. Mix in the brown sugar and the eggs.

Pulse to a smooth and creamy batter. Stir in two-thirds of the apple mixture. Spoon the batter into the springform pan and sprinkle with the rest of the apple mixture. Sprinkle with the raw cane sugar.

Bake the cake for about 50 minutes, until done. When in doubt, pierce with a skewer; if it comes out dry, the cake is ready.

Let cool somewhat on a rack before removing the springform and serving.

makes 1 cake

14 ounces (400 g) apples, peeled and cored

Juice of ½ lemon

Generous ¾ cup (125 g) raisins

⅓ cup (75 ml) dark rum

1 teaspoon ground ginger

1 teaspoon ground cinnamon

½ teaspoon ground cloves

Pinch of sea salt

FOR THE BATTER

1 teaspoon ground cinnamon

9 tablespoons (125 g) butter, at room temperature

1¾ cups (225 g) self-rising flour

½ cup plus 1 tablespoon (125 g) packed dark brown sugar

3 small or 2 large eggs

3 tablespoons raw cane sugar

PREHEAT THE OVEN
TO 250°F (125°C)
CAREFULLY CHECK
THE OVEN
THERMOMETER.

HEAT MILK
TOGETHER
WITH VANILLA
BEANS & STARANISE.
(OR ORANGE ZEST, CARDEMOM,
OR... OR....)

BEAT EGG YOLKS,
SUGAR & HEAVY.
CREAM, POUR IN
THE HOT MILK.

POUR INTO RAMEKINS

BAKE THEM "LOW & SLOW"
"AU BAIN MARIE"

TOP WITH CRISPY
CARAMELIZED
SUGAR

A great chef once said: "Can she make crème brûlée? Then she can cook." That chef ended up having dinner at the restaurant I owned at the time, and crème brûlée was on the menu. I immediately understood what he meant. It seems like such a simple dish, but that's deceptive; if the oven gets too hot, the egg will solidify too fast and the crème will crumble. If the oven is too cold, the crème will stay runny. Having the right egg-to-liquid ratio is also crucial, but you will learn that information from the following recipe. Naturally, after reading my remarks about ovens on page 177, you all bought oven thermometers, so here we go. We'll make something tasty with *some* level of difficulty. You can do it!

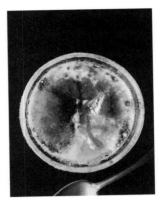

makes 7 to 8 ramekins

- 1 cup plus 1 tablespoon (250 ml) milk
- 1 vanilla bean, split and scraped
- 3 pieces star anise
- Butter for greasing the ramekins
- 5 egg yolks
- ¾ cup (150) g sugar
- 1 cup plus 1 tablespoon (250 ml) heavy cream

STAR ANISE CRÈME BRÛLÉE

Heat the milk to a near boil. Add the vanilla seeds and bean, and the star anise. Let steep over low heat for 15 minutes.

Preheat the oven to 250°F (125°C). Grease 7 or 8 ramekins with some butter.

Beat the egg yolks with half of the sugar. Beat in the cream and then the hot milk. Pour into the ramekins. Place all of them inside a large baking dish. Carefully place in the oven. Pour in boiling water, half submerging the ramekins, and bake for 1 hour and 15 minutes, until firm. Let the crème brûlées cool on the counter, then cover and refrigerate so they'll become ice cold and solidify.

Before serving, set the broiler to high. Sprinkle the ramekins with the remaining sugar and slide under the hot broiler until caramelized. Naturally you can also do this with a real crème brûlée torch if you have one. Serve.

HOLLOW OUT
SOME CRISP APPLES.
A MELON BALLER WORKS
BEST FOR THIS.

A SMALL SCOOP WITH
A SHARP EDGE & A
TINY HOLE IN THE MIDDLE.

LEAVE THE
BOTTOM INTACT!

COVER WITH
A LATTICEWORK
OF DOUGH!
(OR SOME OTHER
DESIGN WITH
CUT-OUT STARS
OR SOMETHING.
WHATEVER YOU
LIKE → BAKE!

SO
YUM!

Not too long ago I received a basket of old-fashioned Jonagolds. I knew they were cooking apples, but nevertheless I tried them out in the following recipe. Naturally I failed because, yes, Jonagold *is* a cooking apple, so they burst apart. Their flavor is of an unsurpassed tartness. I made the recipes again but this time combining Grannies (a bit more sour) with Elstars (a bit sweeter). Turned out great. I could've used winesap, but those are even sweeter. What's most important is that the apples stay firm when baked, because in these tartlets the apple itself forms the crust instead of the filling. Funny, right?

Less suitable as baking apples are varieties such as Jonagold, Pink Lady, Braeburn, Gala, Delicious, or Junami. However, those are perfect for eating out of hand because they tend to be juicier.

APPLE TARTLETS

Preheat the oven to 400°F (200°C).

Use a melon baller to remove the core from the apples and then enough of the pulp so you are left with a shell ¼ inch (½ cm) thick inside the peel.

Finely chop the pulp and mix with the lemon juice and then with the brown sugar, spices, and salt. Stuff the apples with the mixture; this is easiest with your (washed!) hands.

Cut the puff pastry into thin strips. Place them over the stuffed opening of each apple, woven like lattice; four strips in either direction. Brush with beaten egg. Place the apples in a baking dish, pour in the cider or water, and cover with aluminum foil.

Bake for 20 minutes, then remove the foil and bake for another 20 to 25 minutes, until golden brown. The apples should be just done but not popped yet. Serve.

makes 4 tartlets

Butter for the bowl

4 large or 6 small apples: Elstar, Granny Smith, or Cox

1 tablespoon fresh lemon juice

5 tablespoons (70 g) packed dark brown sugar

1 tablespoon flour

½ teaspoon ground cinnamon

½ teaspoon ground allspice

¼ teaspoon freshly grated nutmeg

Pinch of ground cloves

Pinch of sea salt

2 5-inch (12-cm) square sheets all-butter puff pastry

1 egg, beaten

Splash of cider or apple juice (optional)

WHAT DO YOU
MAKE WITH YOGURT
LEMON & GINGER?

THE RIGHT ANSWER IS : CAKE

COMBINE: ALL-PURPOSE FLOUR,
ALMOND FLOUR, LEMON ZEST,
GRATED GINGER, SUGAR,
BAKING POWDER & SALT.

BEAT: EGGS
SUNFLOWER OIL
& YOGURT

COMBINE EVERYTHING.
POUR INTO A SPRINGFORM PAN
→→→ →B A K E←← ←←←

I just returned from a food getaway in southern Italy. People there are such good cooks that experimenting at home in our vacation rental made no sense at all. So we filled our bellies with local specialties. And because there were so many, we spent all day doing so.

Back home I was overcome by an enormous baking urge. After sitting on my hands for so long I was itching to fire up the oven, but the only ingredients I had were an old carton of yogurt and a neglected ginger root. Luckily that was sufficient for an excellent cake.

YOGURT CAKE WITH LEMON & GINGER

Preheat the oven to 350°F (180°C). Grease an 8-inch (20 cm) springform pan and line the bottom with parchment paper cut to size.

In a mixing bowl, combine the flours, lemon zest, ginger, brown sugar, baking powder, and salt. In a pitcher, whisk the eggs, oil, and yogurt together.

Form a well in the middle of the dry ingredients and pour in the contents of the pitcher. Fold everything together with a spoon. Don't whisk: If you do, the cake won't become crumbly and it won't rise as well, either.

Pour into the springform pan and bake for 40 minutes, or until a skewer comes out dry.

Meanwhile, make the syrup: Slowly boil all of the ingredients plus ⅓ cup (75 ml) water for 10 minutes. Strain and set aside.

Let the cake rest for 5 minutes, then remove from the springform pan. Place on a rack and poke holes all over it with a skewer. Drizzle with half of the syrup. Allow to absorb. After an hour, drizzle with the second half. Leave to stand for a bit longer before serving.

makes 1 cake

⅓ cup plus 1 teaspoon (80 ml) sunflower oil, plus extra for greasing the pan

1 cup plus 6 tablespoons (175 g) self-rising flour

¾ cup plus 2 tablespoons (100 g) almond flour

Grated zest of 2 lemons

4 inches (10 cm) fresh ginger, peeled and grated

⅔ cup plus 1 tablespoon (150 g) packed light brown sugar

1½ teaspoons baking powder

Pinch of sea salt

2 eggs

Scant 1 cup (225 ml) plain yogurt

FOR THE SYRUP

Scant ½ cup (100 g) packed light brown sugar

Juice of 2 lemons

2½ inches (6 cm) fresh ginger, peeled and grated

My sister and I have a lifelong food-gifting agreement. When one of us goes on vacation she will bring the other a bag full of edible goodies that are local to the country. These presents are then to be offered with the words "I just brought you a little something, nothing special," but these gifts are never trifles. The fennel seeds I brought my sister from Le Marche in Italy are so much more aromatic and greener than the ones from the local Dutch supermarket. Same with the presents she brought me from Sardinia—real bottarga made from grey mullet (like it should be), exquisitely wrapped almond candy, and a package of pistachio flour. Try finding that at home. Such gifts are simply priceless. I used the latter to make financiers—buttery French cakes that immediately turned out tastier than all of the ones I had made with almond flour. You can make your own flour by grinding roasted pistachios in a food processor. Go ahead, try it.

makes about 15 cakes

- 11 tablespoons (150 g) butter, plus extra for greasing the pans
- 7 tablespoons (50 g) all-purpose flour
- 1½ cups (150 g) sifted confectioners' sugar
- ½ teaspoon sea salt
- ½ cup (60 g) ground pistachio flour
- 3 egg whites
- ½ cup (70 g) blackberries, blueberries, or raspberries

PISTACHIO FINANCIERS

In a saucepan, melt the butter over medium heat until the milk solids start browning and sink to the bottom of the pan, while the butter fat becomes clear and turns a nice deep caramel color. The whole process takes about 15 minutes. Remove from the heat.

Preheat the oven to 400°F (200°C).

In a bowl, combine the all-purpose flour, confectioners' sugar, salt, and pistachio flour. Add the melted butter (the milk solids should remain in the saucepan, but don't worry if a few slip through), and egg whites and stir everything to a smooth batter using a spatula.

Pour the batter into greased mini cake molds, divide the blackberries among them, and bake for about 12 minutes (depending on the size of your cake molds; make sure to check!), until golden brown.

After letting them cool for 5 minutes, you can eat them.

Note: Pistachio flour really shines in this recipe, but feel free to substitute almond or hazelnut flour, if you'd like. You won't get the same flavor as you do with pistachio flour, but the financiers will still be delicious.

PEANUT
BUTTER

DARK
BROWN
SUGAR

SUGAR

ALMOND
MEAL

2 EGGS

2 T.S.P
BAKING
POWDER

COMBINE ALL INGREDIENTS
INTO A DOUGH BALL.

SHAPE INTO LITTLE BALLS.
PLACE THEM,
WELL SPACED
ON A BAKING
SHEET.

FLATTEN
WITH A
COOKIE STAMP
OR FORK.

SPRINKLE WITH
FLAKY
SALT

BAKE FOR 8 TO 10 MINUTES
— LET COOL —

Peanut butter is hip. I noticed this because I have six jars of it in my cupboard. And none of these I bought myself. Many of the jars have a fashionable, retro look, and their labels scream how they contain zero artificial additives; pure and unadulterated. Well, sometimes they have some added sea salt or extra chunky nuts, but that's it. Their producers are sending them to me nonstop. So it's time to finally use them. I may not be your typical peanut butter sandwich eater, but I do bake cookies. So that's what I did; I made peanut cookies. *With* almond and sea salt, but without gluten (nice to know perhaps for those fashionable people with a gluten-phobia).

PEANUT ALMOND COOKIES

Preheat the oven to 350°F (180°C). Line two large baking sheets with parchment paper or silicone mats.

Swiftly mix all the ingredients except the flaky salt together to make a non-sticky dough. Using clean hands, roll little balls the size of walnuts and place them on the baking sheets, spaced a little apart (they will spread considerably).

Press them with a cookie stamp, with those silicone prints (available in baking or home goods stores), or using a fork into round flat cookies. Sprinkle with the salt flakes.

Bake the cookies in the middle of the oven (one sheet at a time) for 8 to 10 minutes, until nicely browned. Stay around because this will go pretty fast. Allow the cookies to cool somewhat before removing them from the baking sheet and letting them cool further on a rack.

They'll still be soft when they come out of the oven but will become crunchy after cooling off.

makes 32 cookies

Scant 1 cup (250 g) peanut butter

½ cup plus 1 tablespoon (125 g) packed dark brown sugar

½ cup plus 2 tablespoons (125 g) granulated sugar

1 cup plus 1 tablespoon (125 g) almond flour

2 eggs

2 teaspoons baking powder

Pinch of sea salt

1 tablespoon flaky salt

LEFTOVER EGG WHITES?
MAKE FINANCIERS!

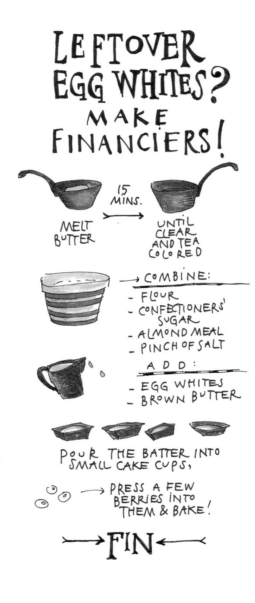

MELT BUTTER

15 MINS.

UNTIL CLEAR AND TEA COLORED

COMBINE:
- FLOUR
- CONFECTIONERS' SUGAR
- ALMOND MEAL
- PINCH OF SALT

ADD:
- EGG WHITES
- BROWN BUTTER

POUR THE BATTER INTO SMALL CAKE CUPS,

PRESS A FEW BERRIES INTO THEM & BAKE!

FIN

After making a bowl of custard I had a bowl of egg whites left over. This kind of thing probably happens to you, too. With those remaining egg whites, you can make financiers. Financiers are feather-light little cakes made with brown butter and nut flour. They are so delicious that I need to control myself not to wolf down the entire platter at once. Brown butter is also known as *beurre noisette*, and it's delicious with everything: fish, for example, or steamed broccoli, or in a pilaf. Its quality mostly stands out in these little cakes, though, and you can make them in no time.

On the next page, you'll find a festive Christmas dessert for any remaining egg whites, because I had even more leftover.

makes about 15 cakes

- 11 tablespoons (150 g) butter, plus extra for greasing the pans
- 7 tablespoons (50 g) all-purpose flour
- 1½ cups (150 g) sifted confectioners' sugar
- ½ cup (60 g) almond flour, hazelnut flour, or ground pistachios
- Pinch of sea salt
- 3 egg whites
- ½ cup (70 g) blueberries (or raspberries)

FiNANCiERS WiTH BLUEBERRiES

In a saucepan, melt the butter over medium heat until the milk solids start browning and sink to the bottom of the pan, while the butter fat becomes clear and turns a nice deep caramel color. The entire process takes about 15 minutes. Remove from the heat.

Preheat the oven to 400°F (200°C).

In a bowl, combine the all-purpose flour, confectioners' sugar, almond flour, and salt. Add the melted butter (the milk solids should remain in the saucepan, but don't worry if a few slip through) and the egg whites and stir everything to a smooth batter using a spatula.

Pour the batter into greased mini cake molds, arrange the berries on top, and bake for about 12 minutes (depending on the size of your cake molds; make sure to check!), until golden brown.

After letting them cool for 5 minutes, you can eat them.

MAKING PAVLOVA ISN'T THAT HARD!

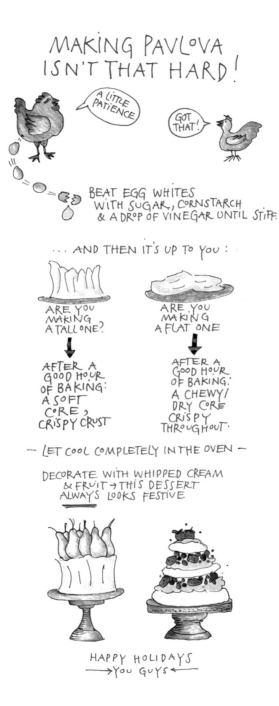

A LITTLE PATIENCE

GOT THAT!

BEAT EGG WHITES WITH SUGAR, CORNSTARCH & A DROP OF VINEGAR UNTIL STIFF.

... AND THEN IT'S UP TO YOU:

ARE YOU MAKING A TALL ONE?

ARE YOU MAKING A FLAT ONE

AFTER A GOOD HOUR OF BAKING: A SOFT CORE, CRISPY CRUST

AFTER A GOOD HOUR OF BAKING: A CHEWY/ DRY CORE CRISPY THROUGHOUT.

— LET COOL COMPLETELY IN THE OVEN —

DECORATE WITH WHIPPED CREAM & FRUIT → THIS DESSERT ALWAYS LOOKS FESTIVE

HAPPY HOLIDAYS → YOU GUYS ←

Pavlova is a crowd-pleaser, and therefore a great dessert for your Christmas dinner. In fact, it's not too difficult. You use 4½ tablespoons (55 g) sugar per egg white, and add a bit of cornstarch and vinegar for a nice soft center and a crunchy exterior. There's also cornstarch in confectioners' sugar. This keeps the meringue nicely stiff. Just don't open the oven while baking. Look through the window. A pavlova cracks; it should crack, so it can't really fail. You can make it a day in advance, but don't keep it in the fridge. Store it in the cold oven instead: Meringue doesn't like humidity.

Merry Christmas!

SOFT BROWN PAVLOVA

Preheat the oven to 400°F (200°C). Line a baking sheet with parchment paper.

Whip the egg whites in a clean, grease-free bowl. While whipping, add the cornstarch, vinegar, and salt.

Combine the sugars. When the egg white is almost stiff, spoon in the sugar, continuing to whip, adding the next spoon only once the previous one has been absorbed entirely. Continue whipping until the mixture is stiff and shiny.

Spoon everything into a big circle on the parchment-lined baking sheet, generously piled high. With the back of a spoon, create pretty curls along the sides.

Bake the pavlova for 10 minutes, then lower the oven temperature to 210°F (100°C) and bake for another good hour. Turn off the oven and let dry in the oven for at least 2 hours.

Fill with a mixture of whipped cream and sour cream (if you wish, you can add a splash of liqueur).

Arrange the fruit over the cream and possibly add strings of melted chocolate or a dusting of confectioners' sugar and serve.

makes 1 pavlova; serves about 8

5 egg whites

1 tablespoon cornstarch

1 scant tablespoon vinegar

Pinch of sea salt

1 cup (125 g) confectioners' sugar

⅔ cup (150 g) packed dark brown sugar

AND ALSO

½ cup (125 ml) heavy cream, whipped

1¼ cups (300 ml) sour cream

Splash of coffee liqueur or brandy (optional)

About 1 pound 9 ounces (700 g) stewed pears, berries, or bananas

3¼ ounces (90 g) melted chocolate, or confectioners' sugar (optional)

GRIND A BATCH OF NUTS & DARK CHOCOLATE INTO COARSE CRUMBS.

A FOOD PROCESSOR COMES IN HANDY, OTHERWISE YOU'LL BE CHOPPING FOREVER.

PUT THE MIXTURE IN A BOWL, ADD COGNAC, DARK BROWN SUGAR, YOLKS & ORANGE ZEST.

beat EGG WHITES STIFF AND FOLD THEM IN.

SCOOP THE BATTER INTO A GREASED BAKING PAN. BAKE! MERRY, MERRY!

This is an addictive dessert cake that, aside from the fact that it's insanely easy to make, has a couple other advantages: It can be made in advance (even up to two weeks!). It's gluten free, almost lactose free, and on top of that it's simply very good. You may actually please practically everyone at your Christmas dinner table. I like it with a scoop of ice cream or a rich crème fraîche, but I leave that to you. By the way, if you make it early and you find the cake a little dry when serving, poke a few holes in it with a fine skewer and drizzle it with some liquor.

CHOCOLATE NUT CAKE

makes 1 cake

Baking spray or olive oil

7 ounces (200 g) dark chocolate (at least 70 to 75 percent cacao), in chunks

14 ounces (400 g) unsalted nuts (hazelnuts, pecans, pistachios)

5 eggs, separated

Grated zest of 1 orange

⅓ cup (75 ml) cognac

¾ cup plus 2 tablespoons (200 g) packed dark brown sugar

Pinch of sea salt

1 tablespoon cocoa powder, to decorate

Preheat the oven to 340°F (170°C). Grease an 8½-inch (22 cm) springform pan with baking spray or oil.

In a food processor, grind the chocolate and the nuts into coarse crumbs. If you don't have a machine, you'll have to chop them by hand.

Pour the choco-nut crumb into a bowl, combine with the egg yolks, orange zest, cognac, and brown sugar and stir until you have a smooth mix. Whip the egg whites and salt until nearly stiff (too stiff results in a dry cake!) in a clean, grease-free bowl. Working in batches, fold the egg whites swiftly into the chocolate mass, making sure that as much air as possible remains in the mixture.

Scoop into the springform pan and bake for 35 minutes, or until a skewer inserted into the middle comes out clean.

Let cool, and sprinkle with cocoa powder before serving.

HOLIDAY LEFTOVERS PIE

THROW IN THE ENTIRE XMAS GIFT BOX

1 JAR OF PICKLED GINGER

BOTTLE OF PRETENTIOUS LIQUOR

BAG OF FANCY NUTS

CONFECTIONERS' SUGAR.

LOST TANGERINES FROM THE FRUIT BOWL

LEFTOVER POLENTA

DECORATE THE CAKE WITH FLOWERS FROM THE CHRISTMAS CENTRE PIECE!

If you're like me, you've probably bought too many groceries for the holidays. Often these are the kind of ingredients you won't want to see, or can't use, after the holidays. So we'll make a festive New Year's Eve cake from all of that. A new cake, made from old stuff, that also clears out your pantry. A jar of stem ginger, for example, a pack of confectioners' sugar, a few fingers of liquor, and a bag of sliced almonds or hazelnuts, I know just what to do with those. Everything can go, hop, into the cake. Delicious. Be merry!

GINGER-ORANGE PANTRY-CLEARING CAKE

Cook the oranges in a large saucepan of water for 1 hour.

Let them cool slightly and process them whole in a food processor, along with the lemon juice, almonds, and three-quarters of the ginger, to a smooth pulp. Stir in the polenta, baking powder, and vanilla sugar. With a hand mixer, beat the eggs with the plain granulated sugar in another bowl until the mixture is a thick white foam.

Preheat the oven to 350°F (180°C). Generously grease a 9-inch (23 cm) springform pan, line the bottom with parchment paper cut to fit, and grease the paper.

Fold the polenta-orange mixture gently into the egg mixture and scoop it into the springform pan.

Bake for about 1 hour, until evenly browned on top and a toothpick inserted in the center comes out clean. Let cool in the pan for 5 minutes, then remove from the pan and let cool entirely on a rack.

You can pour some liquor over the cake while it's cooling, if you'd like. Stir the ginger syrup into the confectioners' sugar until it's a thick glaze, pour over the cake, and decorate with the remaining ginger, thinly sliced.

makes 1 cake

2 large oranges (or 3 to 4 clementines), scrubbed with hot water

Juice of 1 lemon

1 cup (100 g) almond flour

1 (8¾-ounce/250 g) jar stem ginger, drained, syrup reserved

½ cup (70 g) coarse polenta

1 teaspoon baking powder

1 teaspoon vanilla extract

6 eggs

1¼ cups (250 g) granulated sugar

Butter for greasing the pan

FOR ON TOP

About 1 tablespoon cognac or whiskey (if you like)

Syrup from the ginger jar (about ⅓ cup/75 ml)

2½ cups (250 g) sifted confectioners' sugar

I digress from my oven theme for a real traditional Dutch New Year's Eve recipe. This is to prevent you from having to scramble to find a good recipe, as they are always impossible to find when you need them. Personally, I'm a fan of apple beignets—the tart apple cuts through the greasy doughnut around it. An apple beignet is better balanced. If you really don't like them, then omit the apples and fold ¾ cup (125 g) of raisins, steeped (in rum!), into the batter before you let it rise—then they'll turn into the traditional Dutch doughnuts (*oliebollen*). If you wish, you can replace the cinnamon sugar with confectioners' sugar. You can go any which way you want; it's your party.

Wishing you a great New Year's Eve.

APPLE BEIGNETS WITH CINNAMON SUGAR

Combine the lukewarm milk with the yeast and 3 tablespoons of the sugar. Let stand for 10 minutes. Sift the flour and salt into a bowl. Make a well in the center and break the egg into it. Using a hand mixer, whisk in the milk-yeast mixture. Add some more milk, if necessary.

Let the batter rise for 1 hour in a warm place.

Heat the oil in a deep pot or deep-fryer to 350°F (180°C).

Dip an apple slice into the batter and slide it into the hot oil. Fry three or four beignets at a time and flip them after a few minutes. Depending on their thickness they'll need about 6 minutes total.

Combine the remaining 6 tablespoons (75 g) sugar with the cinnamon in a shallow bowl. Let the beignets drain for a bit on paper towels, then dip them into the cinnamon sugar on both sides. Serve warm.

makes 16 to 20 beignets

2 cups plus 2 tablespoons (500 ml) lukewarm milk

4½ teaspoons (2 envelopes/ 14 g) instant yeast

9 tablespoons (110 g) sugar

4 cups (500 g) all-purpose flour

Pinch of sea salt

1 egg

3 to 4 tart apples (such as Cortland), peeled, cored with a melon baller, and cut into thick slices

Peanut oil, for deep-frying

1 tablespoon ground cinnamon

CHOCOLATE NUT CAKE, PAGE 193

BLACKBERRY RICOTTA CAKE, PAGE 171

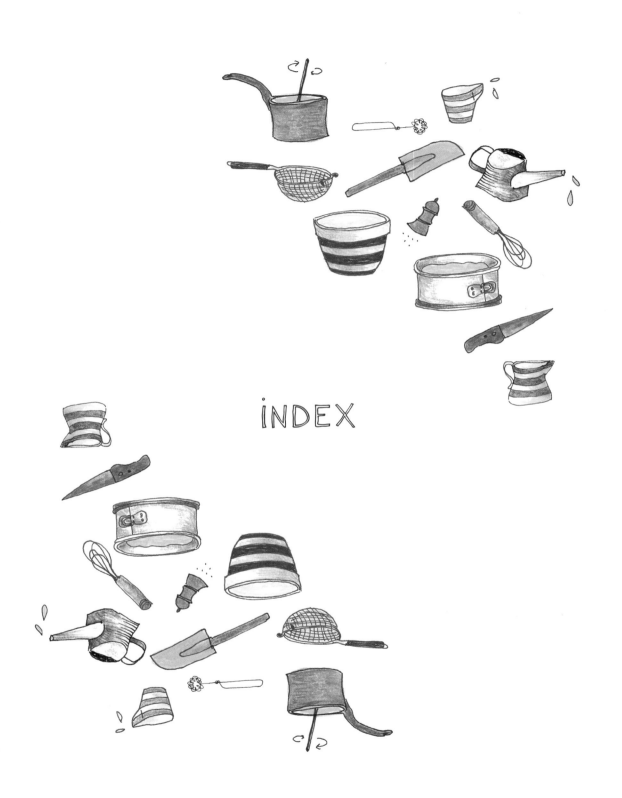

INDEX

INDEX BY CHAPTER

INDEX BY INGREDIENT

RHUBARB BEET SALAD, PAGE 57